ENGAGING YOUR POWER

ENGAGING YOUR POWER

Using Your Divine Energy to Have the Life You Want

Mary Ann Robbat

iUniverse, Inc.
Bloomington

Engaging Your Power
Using Your Divine Energy to Have the Life You Want

iUniverse books may be ordered through booksellers or by contacting:

iUniverse
1663 Liberty Drive
Bloomington, IN 47403
www.iuniverse.com
1-800-Authors (1-800-288-4677)

ISBN: 978-1-4620-2195-6 (sc)
ISBN: 978-1-4620-2197-0 (hc)
ISBN: 978-1-4620-2198-7 (e)

Library of Congress Control Number: 2011908296

Printed in the United States of America

iUniverse rev. date: 07/27/2011

To Zoe, Luke and Maya who always shine their light where ever they go.

To Matt who has always encouraged, supported and helped me on my journey. I love you.

A special thanks to all of my clients who without you I wouldn't keep delving deeper into this work. To some special friends, who certainly know who they are, thank you for your love, commitment and support. A super special thanks to Di Hall, Stacey Coombs, and Matt who worked with me intensely in the editing phase of this book. To my large extended family who keep me grounded and rooted in the important connections of life.

Table of Contents

Notes from the Author

Over many years of doing coaching and energy work with clients, I began to get a clear picture of how much our belief systems either help or hinder us in life. These beliefs, sometimes conscious and sometimes unconscious, control our lives. I began to look at the energy behind a client's beliefs to see how hard it would be to change those beliefs. The key I found in working with clients was that the more conscious we are of our beliefs, the easier it is to feel how to welcome and keep them (because the beliefs are working for us) or release them (because they get in our way).

It is our subconscious beliefs that challenge us and create stuck energy in our systems. Studying and performing energy healing with many clients helped me become aware of how connected our beliefs are with our energy systems. Every belief, conscious and subconscious, also resides in our energy systems. If we try to mindfully change beliefs through affirmations, we have only a fifty-fifty chance of succeeding if we don't work with our energy systems as well.

I have seen first-hand that changing a belief without releasing the energy of the belief doesn't always work. You must change a belief, find the energy of the belief, and release it to be successful.

I also had clients who were making changes to their beliefs and energy with results that were less than I expected. It wasn't until I explored their beliefs around "deserving" and connected this to their ability to manifest that I found the last subsystem of the Success Triad. I realized that our ability to manifest is affected when we have confusion about the following questions:

- How much can I have?
- What is too much? What is too little?
- Do I deserve this? Am I being greedy?

~

My journey on the path to energy healer was not an obvious one, at least, at first, not to me. Born the fifth of six children in a middle class family, I was extremely intuitive at a young age. At around fourteen years old, a series of confusing circumstances scared me away from my spiritual healer path, and I put my intuitive abilities aside to focus on the "normal" path of a formal education and career.

After graduating from college, I worked in the high tech industry for almost twenty years. Over that time, I held many different titles and played many different roles, primarily focused on enabling people and businesses to see and realize their full potential. I developed programs to support individual and organizational growth. I worked to create change, revitalize organizations, and transition to new visions and cultures.

But my path has not been a straight one, or narrowly focused on business. At the age of twenty-seven, I met a success coach and began working with her to determine what I wanted in all aspects of my life. I loved doing this work. It helped me identify my true purpose in life—to heal, teach, and guide—and brought clarity and focus that enabled me to begin to fully live my life in and from my purpose. I was impressed with the power of the program. My coach thought I would make a great success coach and encouraged me to take the certification program. After completing it, I began my part-time career as a success coach while continuing to work full-time in the high tech industry. I found this coaching work to be extremely effective and very personally rewarding. I witnessed people making significant changes in their lives.

At the age of twenty-eight, I met a shaman through my corporate work who changed my life. He put me back in touch with my intuition and showed me how to access my personal guides in the spiritual world. This was all strange stuff for the rational East Coast back in the 1980s, but I felt compelled to learn as much as possible.

While I continued on my corporate career path, I also opened up my spiritual path and began investigating and using the hidden gifts and talents from my childhood that I had reawakened.

I learned how to psychically connect to an individual's soul and deliver its messages. I learned about the chakra energy system in the body and how to release old energy and bring in new energy. Over the course of ten years, I studied with four additional shamans to learn many disciplines in spiritual modalities as diverse as Reiki, shamanism, and Eastern practices in the study of meridian points. I began yearly journeys to rural areas of Peru to work with indigenous shamans. As time went on, the shamans were as eager to work with me and learn of my spiritual connections as I was to learn about theirs.

Although learning these many disciplines broadened my knowledge and experience, I have always trusted and prioritized my own intuition and worked with my spiritual guides to determine what is best for my clients.

While I was working full-time in the high tech industry and coaching clients on nights and weekends, a miracle happened: I gave birth to three wonderful children – triplets! Needless to say, I had to make room for this new full-time responsibility, which meant some of my existing responsibilities had to go.

My decision was easy. Although I was very competent and knew the world of business well, my passion was clearly around coaching private clients. I also wanted to explore the healer I was becoming. At the age of forty-two, I "retired" from my corporate career and focused exclusively on my coaching and spiritual healer path.

This book is my opportunity to share with you the powerful Success Triad so that many more people can live the lives they desire.

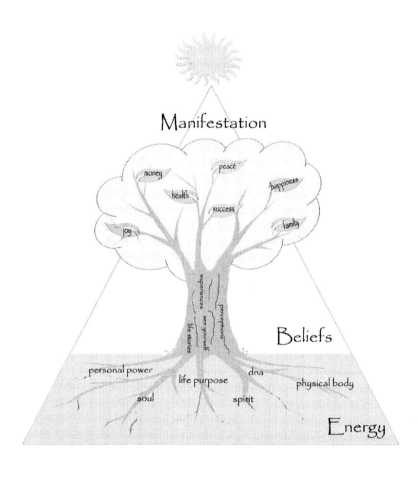

Manifestation

money
peace
health
happiness
success
joy
family

experiences
perceptions
see yourself
life stories

Beliefs

personal power
life purpose
dna
physical body
soul
spirit

Energy

Success Triad

Introduction

Patterns and beliefs emerge from within people's stories that prove to either help them realize and live the lives they desire or stop them cold from getting what they want.

As an energy healer, I have been addressing the intellectual and spiritual needs of my clients, on both the conscious and subconscious levels, for more than twenty years. After working with many people from all walks of life—CEOs, executives, artists, engineers, health caregivers, mothers, fathers, sons, daughters—I have found that successful, long-term transformation occurs when three major factors are brought into alignment: energy, beliefs, and the ability to manifest or create things in life.

I have watched clients with a strong desire to quit their financially secure but lifeless jobs successfully take on such financially risky careers as art and writing. I have supported clients in transforming marginal relationships into thriving ones. I have seen them truly love the lives they have created for themselves.

My clients are a diverse group of men and women who have one thing in common: they want to make changes to live more expansive and satisfying lives. After working in the business world for twenty years and running my own healing practice for the last twelve, I'm convinced that the concepts I will introduce to you will work within any domain or facet of your life.

This book is about the method I created and evolved through working with my clients. I call it the Success Triad, and it is based on spiritual laws I have come to understand through years of reflection and real world practice. As you will see, working with only one or two of the major factors can create real, important change in your life, but working with all three is by far the most powerful and best way to achieve long-term results.

This book has three main goals:

1. To describe the Success Triad, which consists of your Energy, Belief, and Manifestation Systems and how these three major systems are interrelated and necessary to create the life you want.

2. To assist you in shifting beliefs that are keeping you stuck, encourage you to unleash your energy so it works for you, and guide you in becoming a powerful "manifestor,"— one who can create for yourself what you truly want.

3. To provide exercises to help you learn to master and support these three systems.

You can use the Success Triad if you are having challenges in your life, such as the following:

- Feeling stuck
- Being unable to manifest what you desire
- Experiencing illness in your body
- Experiencing challenges in your career
- Being depressed
- Having a lack of financial abundance

- Having low energy
- Lacking intimate relationships
- Living in unfulfilling relationships
- Feeling little or no support in your life
- Feeling overwhelmed

You can also use the Success Triad when your life is going in the direction you desire but you seek more, such as the following:

- A higher level of connection with spirit
- Guidance on your spiritual journey
- Strengthened body, mind, and spirit
- A higher level of fulfillment in life

I am excited to share the Success Triad with you and show you how to use it to create effective, long-term change. The Success Triad and its interrelated systems will lead you to engage your power, the truest expression of who you want to be in this lifetime, and what you want to experience.

Overview of the Success Triad

This book is organized around the Energy, Belief, and Manifestation Systems, which together form the Success Triad. Each of the three systems is capable of standing alone as well as working with the others. Even though change is possible through working with one of the systems, the probability for lasting change is increased dramatically when you work with all three.

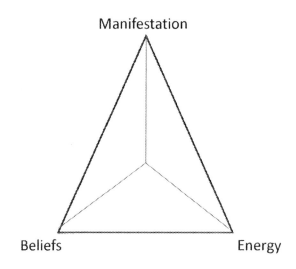

1. Energy System
2. Belief System
3. Manifestation System

I like to use a tree as a metaphor to help you visualize the Success Triad. At the base of the tree are the roots, which create and sustain the life of the tree. This is equivalent to your Energy System. The trunk of the tree, which helps the tree stand tall and strong, is equivalent to the Belief System. The branches and beautiful leaves of the tree are the result of the tree getting the nourishment it needs and the strength of its trunk. This is equivalent to the Manifestation System.

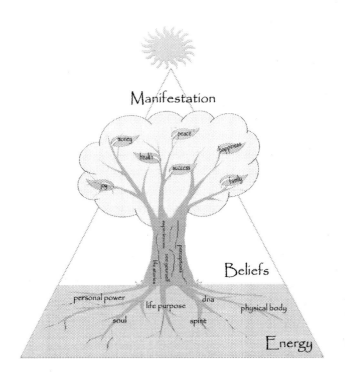

This chapter is an overview of the three systems and their subsystems. Each of the three systems will be covered in more detail in later chapters.

Energy System

Your Energy System is made up of all that you are. It encompasses the following components:

- Your connection to your soul, which resides in the spiritual realm
- The energy that physically runs through your body, keeping you alive (DNA, cellular structure, organs)
- Your ego, which makes you unique in the world

For simplicity, I have broken the Energy System into three subsystems, which exist as energetic fields:

- Spiritual (or Soul) Energy Field
- Life Force Energy Field
- Identity Energy Field

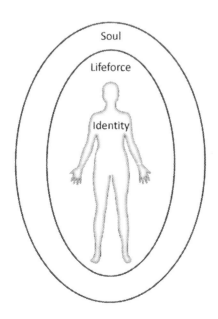

A. **Spiritual Energy Field** – This energy is equivalent to your DNA and is what makes you who you are from birth. It is tied to your spiritual nature. Your life purpose is in this energy center. Here lie the answers to why you came into this particular physical incarnation and what your soul wants to experience in your physical body.

B. **Life Force Energy Field** – This is the energy that drives you, that gets you up in the morning, and that allows your body to run healthfully and smoothly throughout the day. It is connected to your will and is where your mind works. This energy is fed to you from your soul as long as you live on this earth. Everyone's Life Force Energy is unique. Some people have powerful and strong Life Force Energy Fields; you can feel them before they enter a room. Other people's are subtle and softer. Life Force Energy is the energy required to support your body's functioning in order to stay connected to your spiritual energy and fulfill the vision of who you are and what you want in this lifetime

C. **Identity Energy Field** – This energy is how you see yourself in the world. It is made up of your perceptions, experiences, and stories of your life. This is the energy that holds your memories and what you perceive as your reality. This energy always has a positive and a negative feeling attached to it. The experiences you have had in life that feed you, foster you, and help you to see yourself in your greatest light are usually your expansive energy, while the experiences you have had that were painful or hurtful or have limited the way you hold yourself are usually your negative energy.

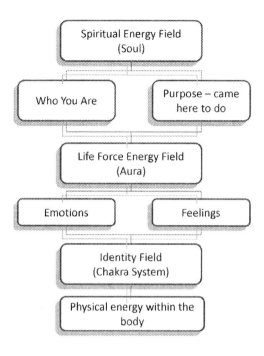

We are all affected by the three subsystems of the Energy System. If we lose our connection to Spiritual Energy, we lose a source of energy that helps inform us of which choices to make to live a life of deep fulfillment. If our Life Force Energy becomes clogged from lack of movement forward in life, we begin to experience many illnesses. The field that mostly drives the way we experience the world is the Identity Energy subsystem. I have clients who can remember experiences going back to when they were two or three years old. These particular experiences still shape who they are today as shown in their thoughts and actions.

If you had a very healthy young life, were surrounded by supportive people, and were frequently appreciated for what you brought into the world, you probably have high self-esteem and may choose to take a lot of risks in life. Positive experiences create positive energy, which certainly helps to build your self-esteem, self-image, and self-knowledge. A powerful self-image and self-esteem give you the confidence to desire what you want and typically to receive it as well.

Similarly, unhealthy experiences and stories you hold that create negative energy tend to follow you throughout your life and affect self-esteem and self-image. Unless you do the work to remove the negative energy that is stored in your body, you may find it more difficult to create and sustain the life you want. This is not to say that negative perceptions alone will hinder you or prevent you from receiving what you want in life; however, negativity may make it more challenging for you. I like to call this negative energy the development of our false or limiting beliefs.

Belief System

The Belief System is responsible for how you operate in the world. It is the home of your values and beliefs about right and wrong and what you know about yourself and the world. You operate your Belief System from both a conscious and an unconscious place. When you are operating from a conscious place, you are clear about what you value and your actions support your beliefs. When you operate from an unconscious place, your actions are usually not in alignment with your values and beliefs. Your entire Energy System feeds your Belief System.

In particular, your Identity Energy Field has a strong influence on your beliefs, which results in beliefs that either empower or limit you in living the life you want.

- Your identity holds a picture of success for you.
- It can permit or prevent you from achieving success.
- Your identity is developed through your experiences, which influence your Belief System.

This begins very early on and continues throughout your life.

For example, I held the energy of being fat. This stemmed from always being heavier than my very, very thin sisters when I was young. My identify beliefs about my body image were set early:

- My body isn't great.
- My body is heavy.
- I will never look good.

When I look back now, I see that all through high school, college, and my corporate career, I was an average-sized woman—not thin, but certainly not fat. I remember that on my wedding day, I was twenty-six years old, weighed 118 pounds, and was sure that I was fat. My "fat girl" energy and beliefs informed my identity and how I continued to see myself. I worked on my body image beliefs for many years, but until I removed the "fat girl" energy from my energy field, I could never truly see myself as thin or average.

This is also the force that is in play when people win the lottery or make huge amounts of money and then lose it all. Typically, these people can't hold onto money because they have some underlying false or limiting belief in their Belief Systems that they do not deserve money or that money is somehow bad or wrong. They may also have some negative energy that needs to be released.

Manifestation System

Your needs and desires inform the choices you make to create the life you want to live. Within the Manifestation System is your ability to manifest the life you desire.

Your Manifestation System is made up of three important abilities:

- To be very clear about what you desire
- To be fully ready to receive what you desire
- To connect with the universal energy to make your request

To have clarity in what you desire is important because you must send clear signals to the universe regarding what you want to receive. If one day you order a hamburger, the next day you change your mind and want a cheeseburger, and the day after that you decide you want to go back to the hamburger but add pickles, you keep yourself in the constant energy of wanting something and not in the energy of receiving what you have decided on.

Once you get clarity on what you desire, you must then be ready to receive it. You may ask for something when deep down you hold the belief you don't deserve it. In this case, the universe tries to deliver what you are asking for, but the "mixed message" may cause it to pass you by.

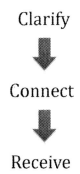

Clarify

Connect

Receive

I learned a very expensive lesson about this dynamic. I always said when I was younger that I wanted to be a millionaire by the time I was forty years old. I didn't want it for the social status that comes with acquiring lots of money. For me, being a millionaire meant freedom in life. I was clear on what I wanted. Years later, the universe delivered to me my millionaire status. I was working for a high tech company in which I had stock options that were worth more than a million dollars. Now, you would think I would thank the universe and run off with the money. However, I also had a number of unconscious beliefs about receiving money that was not directly related to my own "hard" work.

Because these stock options were not directly tied to my personal performance, I never cashed them in for the millions of dollars they were worth. At that time, I didn't know how to receive money I couldn't attribute to my own performance. I also realized, years later of course, that I had no capacity to really envision my life as "easy" and free of financial restrictions. It was a costly lesson but one that led me to explore many of my conscious and unconscious beliefs and also explore my Energy System to find the energetic blocks associated with these beliefs to release them.

Once you are clear about what you desire and you ensure that your beliefs and energy are aligned to receiving it, you must ask the universe to deliver it to you. In this process, you must set a clear intention by making positive statements about receiving what you desire. You can also visualize your life with what you desire as if it were already present and available. Taking it one step further, you can begin to live your life as if you already have it.

Summary

Each of the above systems and subsystems within the Success Triad influences the others. Your personal power system is healthy when all of the subsystems continuously inform and create new beliefs, new energy, new experiences and stories, and new images of yourself that support your overall purpose and goals in life. This will allow you to live the life you desire.

People who live their lives full out are very alive and full of energy, excited about their prospects, at ease with their places in the world, and very attractive to others. It goes beyond material success and is the root of real happiness, joy, and peacefulness. This book seeks to help you create this kind of life for yourself.

The rest of this book is defined by three sections, one for each system in the Success Triad:

- Section 1: Energy System
- Section 2: Belief System
- Section 3: Manifestation System.

Get ready to have some fun. Here we go!

Section 1: Your Energy System

The purpose of introducing you to these energy constructs is to show you the correlation of energy to your beliefs and your identity. I want you to see that it is only through bringing change to the unified Energy System, to all three levels of energy, that you will shift your life toward your desires.

This section is not intended to give you a comprehensive education on the topic of energy. There are numerous definitions of personal energy. In fact, many books are devoted to the in-depth study of your personal energy system, your spiritual energy system, and your etheric energy system. For the purposes of this book, I will define *energy* from my understanding, developed from working within the energy centers and fields for many years. I will also define only the energy systems I believe are critical in doing the work to create the life you truly desire.

We all know what energy is: energy heats our homes, powers our cars, and even helps plants to grow. But the kind of energy I am talking about is our personal energy. This is the energy we use to get out of the bed in the morning and to accomplish what we do in life.

When we see children in parks, some of them run around in constant motion, expending huge amounts of energy in their play. We see other children who sit contentedly playing in the sandbox, using their thoughts and imaginations to build things or make up stories. They are also expending energy. Our thoughts, beliefs, and physical movements are all forms of energy.

We experience people in terms of high energy or low energy. People with high energy tend to be involved in many different activities, believe they can change the state of things, and generally have a positive attitude. People with low energy tend to commit to only what they believe they can do; they limit the possibilities for themselves and live in a state they know they can manage. They tend not to be risk takers or to overcommit themselves. They tend to live from the belief that making it through life is their task rather than from the belief that they can shape life into what they desire.

Our energy gets expressed in more than just movement. It gets expressed in the vocabulary we choose, how we see the world, and our thought patterns. Our attitudes also influence our energy. When we have a generally positive outlook on life, we tend to be more highly energized. Conversely, when we are in a negative thought pattern or belief that life isn't fair or doesn't support us, our energy can be low, and then we tend to sit on the sidelines, cocoon ourselves, and not fully connect to the opportunities in life.

My Work as an Energy Healer/Shaman/Coach

Through the work I do as an energy healer, shaman, intuitive master, and coach, I have had a lot of training and opportunities to work within clients' energy systems. Early on in my career, when I went to various training programs, I would learn about great ways to affect change in one area of a person's energy system or life. I would use these techniques with clients and produce incremental change. However, much of the time, the changes weren't being sustained.

They could bring into their lives what they wanted for a short period, but eventually they would go back to their old ways.

I became curious as to why some clients were having a big impact and were sustainably changing their lives while others were not. What I realized is that all of the energy systems are interrelated. We must take care of all of the systems in order to fully affect change in our lives. For instance, we can't focus only on setting positive intentions and expect results without looking at the beliefs and energy we may hold around a belief that negatively affects our intentions.

Client Study

I had a client once who was clear on what she wanted in a relationship. She could clearly identify the type of man she wanted and how she wanted to be in a relationship with that man. She created her intentions, developed vision boards, and affirmed for herself her ability to attract this man into her life. She was able to meet and date men who met her requirements for a relationship, but she could never stay in the relationship for long.

After a few months of working with her, I noticed a pattern in her ability to attract the man she desired and her inability to make it work. When I looked at the situation from the three energy systems within the Success Triad, I saw that she was working with only two of them. We talked about her ability to emanate the right energy to attract who she wanted, her beliefs, and her manifestation techniques. Her energy, which was high, positive, and focused on wanting a man, was in alignment, and her manifestation processes were also working well. She had a solid practice around saying her intentions, and she created a vision board and affirmed that a man was coming to her.

However, the block resided in her belief system. She remembered times in her life when her dad had told her that she was not the prettiest girl on the block and that she had better settle for the first man who came along. She recalled that her dad would say this jokingly or teasingly to her. Even though there was a level of jest to it, she created a perception about herself. The belief and perception was that she couldn't have a man she chose. She had stored energy and a deep-seated belief that she didn't deserve to have a man of her choosing.

And this played out in her life. She could focus and attract the man she desired, but she would do different things to sabotage the relationship, resulting in the man's leaving. Once we were able to track this memory and the pursuant belief she had created, we were able to release the energy and change her perspective of herself and her belief. It finally freed her up to believe that she could attract and keep the man she desired. I am happy to say that she is now married and has two children.

How to Experience Energy in Your Body

The body's Energy System is a truly complex one. Many books have been written and many distinctions made about our Energy Systems. For the purposes of this book and to help to support you in living the life you desire, I have distilled the Energy System into three primary subsystems:

- Spiritual Energy Field
- Life Force Energy Field
- Identity Energy Field

When I work within a client's Energy System, I look at the three subsystems to identify issues or problem areas. There are three questions I immediately ask as I scan each energy field:

- Is the energy field robust?
- Is it flowing easily?
- Is it connected with a spiritual source?

In scanning for robustness, flow, and connection with spirit, I can usually get a sense of the issues within the Energy System.

For instance, a client can have a robust connection with spirit and a spiritual energy field that is flowing smoothly and strongly. However, when I get to her Identity Energy Field, I may find a number of blocks. It is possible to have a combination of healthy and unhealthy subsystems working simultaneously.

The Spiritual Energy Field

The first field, the Spiritual Energy Field, is the energy that is connected to your soul. This is the energetic field that knows who you are and what you came to do in your human experience. It holds the purpose of your life. When you are flowing in life—meaning you are in a state of happiness and general well-being—you are living from a place of purpose and are in alignment with your spiritual wellness. Usually, when I see illness in this field, it is because a client is ignoring some fundamental need he or she has. Illness first shows up in your Spiritual Energy Field. If you continue to ignore what your soul needs, the illness will appear next in your Life Force Energy Field. And finally, if it continues to go unattended, it will show up in your Identity Energy Field and be evident in symptoms in your physical body.

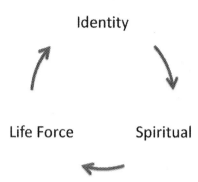

Identity

Life Force   Spiritual

When illness shows up in your Spiritual Energy Field, it is easy to heal. It is like an early-warning system that informs you that illness is near and will manifest in your body if you don't change or shift some of your beliefs, actions, or inactions.

If you are not living your soul's purpose, your Spiritual Energy Field will be cloudy or feel dense. This indicates that the energy between you and your spiritual self is not flowing. Because there is no flow, it is difficult for your spiritual energy to inform you on or help you stay aligned with your life purpose. When the spiritual energy is blocked, you may experience feelings of isolation, restlessness, emptiness, depression, or struggle. These feelings occur because of the energetic disconnect from your higher Spiritual Energy Field.

Exercise: Finding How You Personally Connect or Experience Energy

The best way to learn more about your energy field is to practice feeling and sensing energy. People connect with energy in one of three primary modes:

- Sensing energy
- Seeing energy
- Feeling energy

There is no right, wrong, or best way to work with energy. At this point, it is mainly about understanding your primary mode of connecting to it. And know that it is possible for you to experience the energy in more than one mode.

The following is a simple exercise to help you identify how you connect with energy.

1. Start by placing your hands about six inches apart from each other with your palms facing the ceiling. Imagine a white ball of light on your right hand. Focus on your hand until you can feel, see, or sense this ball of light. Pay attention to how it feels in your palm. Do you feel tingling or lightness, or do you experience the ball of light more as knowing that it is in your palm? Whatever you feel is the exact right thing for you.

2. Now take the ball of light and practice growing the energy of the ball to about six inches in diameter. Once you do this, throw the ball from one hand to the other.

3. You may experience this exercise in several different ways. You may feel the sensations in your hands as the ball leaves one hand and lands in the other. You can feel tingling, the heaviness of the ball, or a buzzing sensation.

4. You may just know when you are throwing the ball when it leaves the first hand and lands in the other. If this is the case

for you, practice throwing the ball faster and faster. See if you can stay in the knowing of when the ball is leaving and arriving in each hand.

5. You may actually see the ball of light in your hand. If this is the case, keep yourself focused on the ball of light and watch it as it leaves one hand and lands in the other. Visualize the ball of light growing or shrinking in your hand.

Once you have a sense of how you feel energy, try the next exercise. It is designed for you to feel the flow of your spiritual energy.

Exercise: Assessing the Flow of Your Spiritual Energy Field

Check your energy for clarity, expansiveness, and ease:

1. First, think about someone or something that makes you joyful or happy.

2. As you continue to think, imagine energy or light flowing from you to the person or thing.

3. Feel, sense, or see how the energy flows from you to the person or thing. Ask yourself these questions:

    • Is the energy flowing easily?
    • Is it flowing quickly or slowly?
    • Does the energy feel light or heavy?

Check your energy for denseness or cloudiness:

1. First, think about a situation that is bothering you, not supporting you, or angering you. Or, think about a person with whom you are upset.

2. As you continue to think, imagine energy or light flowing from you to the person or situation.

3. Feel, sense, or see how the energy flows from you to the person or situation. Ask yourself the same questions:

   • Is the energy flowing easily?
   • Is it flowing quickly or slowly?
   • Does the energy feel light or heavy?

These exercises will help you make the distinctions regarding how your energy shows up when expansive or when stuck. Now, let's check in on your Spiritual Energy Field.

Imagine a big ball of white light or energy in your stomach. Then, move the energy up through your body and out through the top of your head (crown chakra). Create and hold the intention to send this energy to your soul or higher self—the part of you that knows your soul's purpose.

Watch how this energy flows:

   • Is the energy flowing easily?
   • Is it flowing quickly or slowly?
   • Does the energy feel light or heavy?

This will give you a good indication of how your energy is flowing to your Spiritual Energy Field. If you find that the energy is not moving very well or is not all that expansive, exercises later in this chapter will help you release blocked energy and move energy more easily.

The Life Force Energy Field

Life Force Energy can also be described as your aura, which is the second energy field. It is the field that surrounds your body. It can extend anywhere from two to twenty inches from your body, depending on your emotional state. This is where your emotions and feelings surface, showing up as colors surrounding your body. For instance, if you are in a high degree of agitation, a lot of red will be in the energy field around your body. If you are in a peaceful and centered place in your life, there might be a lot of white and violet in your field.

You may have seen photographs or drawings depicting an aura. A special camera can capture the electromagnetic field of your body and thus capture the colors of your field. Some trained healers are able to read auras without any equipment and can supplement a photograph with information gained through a spiritual reading. What is important to know is that the aura is information referring to your Life Force Energy Field at that one moment in time. Your aura is constantly changing as your emotions and feelings change. It is useful to work with your aura because it brings you to the truth of what you are feeling. For instance, you can speak calmly and rationally about a topic while your aura shows colors of distress, contradicting your speaking tone.

This is a good indicator to a healer that you may be holding subconscious thoughts, emotions, or energy that is blocking your conscious awareness.

I work with the aura to check a client's emotional well-being in the moment and to look for energy blocks. When energy blocks appear in the aura, the color may be very dark or there may be an absence of color. The color may also appear only very close to the body or not have a wide span. When this occurs, it informs me that the client's energy is not as expansive as it could be.

I also use the aura to identify areas of abundant energy. When there is an imbalance of energy in the field, it helps me determine if the client is in a high "doing" state or a high "being" state or if he or she is carrying a lot of masculine energy or feminine energy. This energy field is very helpful in informing me about the client's emotional well-being and the level of energy he or she is pulling in. The Life Force Energy and aura are where the flow of the Spiritual Energy Field is visible. If there are blocks in this energy field, it helps me to identify for my clients the places where they may be in discordance with their spiritual selves or life purposes.

Exercise: How to See, Feel, and Sense Your Own Aura

First, remember that your aura represents your own emotional state at one point in time. Emotional states can and do change, so you may get different results with this exercise because of when you practice it.

There are many ways to practice seeing, feeling, and sensing your aura. Below are a few methods I have selected that I believe are the simplest and easiest ways, but they still may require much practice before you can see, feel, or sense your aura. If you are interested in learning more about auras, numerous books on the subject are available.

1. Use your hands to feel the expansiveness of your aura. (Remember that in the previous exercises you began to feel, see, or sense your spiritual energy. Use the same modalities in this exercise.)

2. Hold your hands two to four inches from your body. Move your hands in and out to see, feel, or sense where your aura starts. Your aura may be very subtle; it may take you several attempts to connect with it. Don't give up, though. Just keep trying.

3. Once you have identified where your aura begins, follow the energy out from your body to see, feel, or sense how expansive it is. You can do this by using your hands. You may need to take some steps away from where you are currently standing to follow your aura energy field.

A very expansive aura usually indicates that you are feeling good and that your emotional well-being is balanced. An aura that is tight or condensed around your body usually indicates that your emotional sense of well-being may not be as balanced as it could be.

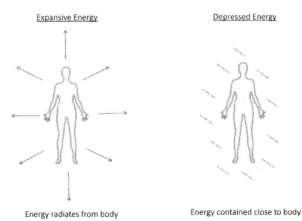

Energy radiates from body   Energy contained close to body

If this is the case, pay attention to what you are thinking and feeling. Perhaps you are holding onto past or present pain—anger, an upset, or hurt feelings. These things will affect your emotional well-being. We will talk later about how to identify and release these past or present pains.

The Identity Energy Field

The third energy field is your Identity Energy Field. Unlike the Life Force Energy Field, which resides outside and around your physical body, this field resides inside your physical body. When I work with this energy field, I use the chakra system (see diagram on the next page) as an organizer and an informer for the energy in the field. The chakra system is a Hindu system that identifies areas of the body that hold specific types of energy. Seven primary chakras reside within the body starting at the top of the head, which is the crown chakra, and ending at the base of the spine, which is the root chakra. These seven primary chakras have certain types of stored energy. You will learn more about the chakra system later in this section, but for now, we will just talk about the third chakra. This is your solar plexus chakra and is where you hold your ability to be powerful in life. This is where your energetic power lives. It provides information about your access to your energetic power. Those who have strong and full access are usually people who can have and do whatever they want in life. People who have weak or partial access walk through life as a victim, fearful and not able to have what they want.

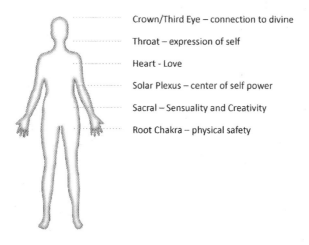

Crown/Third Eye – connection to divine

Throat – expression of self

Heart - Love

Solar Plexus – center of self power

Sacral – Sensuality and Creativity

Root Chakra – physical safety

With my clients, I start by scanning their physical bodies for energy blocks in this field. It is easy for me to determine where the energy is stuck in this field, and when I inform clients of a place where I sense stuck energy, they usually tell me they have some physical ailment, pain, or tightness in that exact region of their bodies.

Client Study

Recently, while giving an intuitive reading to a client, I scanned her chakra system. I realized I couldn't feel energy flowing freely from her head, or crown chakra, beyond her stomach. I could feel the pain and constrictions that were in her third chakra, the solar plexus chakra, which is located in the stomach area of the body. Based on this, I asked her, "What is going on in your stomach?" She told me she had colitis. After finishing the intuitive reading with her, it became very clear to me why she had colitis.

As I said earlier, the solar plexus chakra is where we hold our energetic power. It informs us of our rights, letting us know if we have the right to expect or deserve what we want or have in our lives. In this particular client's intuitive reading, I could see that people in her life were taking her power away by demeaning her and constantly telling her that she was wrong. Added to this, I saw her giving her power away by believing what others were saying and assuming that their opinions were accurate or right and that hers were inaccurate or wrong. This greatly reduced her ability to stand powerfully in the world, honoring and validating her own knowledge.

When we stand fully in our power, we know who we are in the world and are able to freely act confidently from this powerful place. Her shutting down her power energy resulted in a very physical and painful ailment. We worked for many sessions to help her reclaim her power by standing in the possibility that she was accurate or right. We also worked on her being able to voice and express her thoughts and opinions as equal in value to anyone else's. Finally, for full healing to occur, she had to believe in herself—understand that she was worthy and deserved a life she chose for herself. She could do this only by not allowing others' opinions to carry more weight than her own. Once she was able to fully release her care of what others thought about her, she was totally liberated to stand in her power.

Exercise: Scanning Your Solar Plexus Chakra to Release Energy

1. Think about a time in your life when everything was going well for you. You felt on top of the world, and life was turning out just how you imagined or envisioned. If you can't think of such a time in your life, focus on an event or an accomplishment you felt good about.

2. Once you have this time, event, or accomplishment clearly in your mind, relive it. Imagine yourself back in that place and time of your life and relive what happened in as much detail as possible. Do this several times, remembering as much as you can each time.

3. Place your hand about three inches out from your solar plexus chakra and sense how the energy feels. Determine if it is light, heavy, big, small, expansive, contracted, and so on.

4. Move your hand as far away from your body as you can while feeling the energy. Sense how far your energy expands.

5. Check in with your stomach to see how is it feeling. Determine if it feels light, easy, heavy, stuck, and so on.

6. Now, think of a time in your life when you felt powerless. Your powerlessness could have happened for any reason, including the following:

    • You didn't get a job you wanted.
    • You got fired from a job.
    • You didn't get a raise or a promotion.
    • You had a point of view on a topic and nobody listened.
    • You were doing everything you knew how to do and still didn't succeed.
    • Someone ended a relationship with you: a spouse, lover, friend, colleague, or group.
    • Someone berated you or spoke badly about you.
    • You felt rejected.

Once you have this time of powerlessness in mind, go through steps 2–6 above. After completing them, you will know if you have stuck energy. If so, imagine that your hand is a big scooper, and scoop out the energy and place it into a burning candle. Then, imagine the event again but this time with the positive outcome you wanted.

Importance of Working within Your Entire Energy System

When I talk about your Energy System, there are many disciplines and distinctions to consider. The first thing to know is that many cultures, primarily Eastern, have acknowledged and worked within the Energy System for centuries in an effort to create wellness in the physical body. The Chinese focus on "chi" energy; by using acupuncture, energy can be moved to release energy blocks and to allow new energy to flow into the body. Hindis teach the ancient study of chakras, or energy centers found in the body. These chakras correlate to certain parts of the body and also store energy. They open and release energy to create wellness in the body. The Latin American shamans also use chakras as an organizing structure for the energy in the body and work in ways that clear and cleanse the chakras and, therefore, the body, restoring it to wellness.

Only in recent years has Western culture in the United States begun to embrace the idea of energy healing. One of the more familiar energy practices widely accepted here is known as Reiki, which is the practice of allowing the energy to flow through the body to amplify the body's wellness. Many shamans use this practice and much more to release or restore energy. Shamans study where the blocked energy is in the body and know how to help clients remove it. They also work with increasing, enhancing, or changing energy to suit their clients' lives.

I have highlighted the Spiritual, Life Force (aura), and Identity Energy Fields because they correlate with and affect your physical energetic vibration, belief system, and ability to manifest what you want in life. My healing approach is an integration of all three systems because, over many years, I have learned that we must take care of and look after all of them. If I were to work with you, I would see, feel, or sense energy blocks in your body. I would gather more information by using my intuition to tap into your body's knowledge and memory, and then I would use various forms of energy-releasing techniques to help you bring in new energy to heal your body.

The next section is intended to give you enough information to understand how and why you must examine your energy, your entire Energy System, if you really want to change.

How Energy Works in Your Life

Universal Energy

Energy is the most powerful source to help you manifest and live an abundant life. When you use universal energy, you create a two-way communication with the universe, the source that is the creator of all things. You open yourself to receive energy, and you also give energy to the universe. When you are committed to doing your soul's purpose, the power and flow of energy know no bounds. Have you ever noticed that when you are "on" and actively and passionately engaged in your soul's purpose that your life, your relationships, and everything else seem to flow more easily? You feel an abundance of energy, and you "flow," or send, an abundance of energy into the universe.

When you are doing your soul's purpose, your energy flows effortlessly out to the universe and the universe supports this flow of energy by sending it right back to you.

Client Study

I worked with a client once who had trouble getting traction in his work. He was stuck. In our sessions, he talked about doing all the right things as a responsible parent, adult, and professional. He couldn't understand why his business wasn't taking off and the work he had put in wasn't paying off. This was a man who worked fifteen to eighteen hours a day, so it wasn't about work ethic.

I asked him one simple question: "Do you like what you are doing?" He looked at me, shocked by the question. He said this was work; he didn't have to like it. We talked about how he showed up for work for fifteen to eighteen hours a day doing something he didn't enjoy. No wonder he felt stuck!

I talked to him about our personal energy and our soul's passion and purpose—why we are on the planet and living our current lives. I told him that if he focused all of his time and attention on things that did not feed his soul and that he didn't enjoy, he was blocking his flow of energy to the universe. The universe supports us when we are doing the work we are meant to do.

It turns out that he loved both music and art and was very talented in both fields. He used to play guitar in a band, but he quit because it wasn't a "responsible" profession. I asked if he had been successful, and he said that the band had four to five gigs a week. In fact, the original band is still together, with the addition of a new guitarist, and is very popular on the wedding and event circuit. My client is also an extremely talented photographer. He had done some shows in a couple of popular galleries and sold a few pieces a year, even without really trying.

I asked him why he wasn't pursuing these endeavors, and his answer saddened my heart. He said that because he enjoyed them so much, he couldn't possibly do them as work. He had done some of this work that he loved on the side earlier in life, in addition to his full-time marketing job. However, when his twin children came along, he quit them altogether and decided to spend the extra hours working at his corporate job, believing this was the "responsible" thing to do. After working for ten years, he was making good, but not great, money, and he and his wife were able to buy a house; he provided for his family. He thought life was something he had to slug his way through. He found no joy or excitement in life and was depressed. He said the thought of living life like this for another thirty years to retirement felt like a prison sentence.

I asked him who put him in prison. He looked at me, surprised, and said, "All work is like being in prison." He said it was a necessary evil. I told him these were beliefs he held that were draining his Life Force Energy and his will to connect and contribute to life. These were beliefs that were old and unfounded. He needed to decide if he was willing to give up these beliefs.

We spent several sessions working on what he was passionate about. It took us a while to get to the answer because he was so blocked. He had never allowed himself to do work he enjoyed. Once we started to define work that would make him happy, we put goals in place for him to move toward this work. He needed a plan to manifest what he desired.

He took baby steps toward realizing his new goals. Within several months, I noticed a huge improvement in his energy and his excitement for life. He was less depressed, and he became very animated when he talked about the steps he was taking toward his new goals. Over time, he noticed more and more how things would happen almost effortlessly and the right people would show up in his life when he needed them. I call this flow. This is when we are doing our life's work and the universe is supporting us by placing what we need in our paths.

If you are in a place where flow is not happening in your life, ask the following questions:

- Am I passionate about life overall?
- What aspects of life excite, challenge, or fulfill me?
- What aspects feel sluggish, boring, unfulfilling, or, worst case, like a prison sentence?

Exercise: Finding Your Soul's Purpose or Passion in Life

1. Start by remembering times in your life when you felt happy or fulfilled. Think about five to eight different experiences or phases in your life. Think about what you were doing or accomplishing that made you feel this way.

2. List the key activities you were doing and then list how they made you feel. For example, when I built a corporate University program, I had the following feelings:

   - I loved creating a school from inception.

- I loved brainstorming with a group of people to design the most impactful university.
- I loved the teaming aspect of the project.
- I felt a huge sense of accomplishment when the program was up and running.

3. Think about your current job and list things about it that you truly enjoy. List how these activities make you feel.

4. Now list activities in your life that you think of as hobbies or that you allow yourself time to do because you love them. What is special and unique about these things? For example, I love to ski. The activity is skiing, but it is really how it makes me feel that is important.

- I love the sense of freedom I feel every time I head down a slope.
- I love how present I am in each moment because if my mind starts to wander or worry, I tend to fall in the snow.
- I love the physicality of skiing.

5. As your list grows longer, look for repeated patterns in the words you used and see how many times they occur in your list. For instance, on my list, several words kept popping up, such as *creative, creativity, new,* and *accomplishment.* Once you have these key words or phrases, make a list of jobs that would allow you to use the traits or skills in your list of key words. Don't limit yourself on the jobs; just brainstorm. You may also ask others to help you.

6. Once you have a clear idea of activities that you love to do and marketable skills that can be articulated, begin to profile possible jobs that utilize those skills. Some jobs may be in totally new fields, and you may have to do some research to figure out if obtaining one of them would be possible.

7. Write down all the interesting possibilities. Do further research and create a short list of a few jobs to pursue further. You may find that you would need some additional training classes, a certification, or something else. Put a plan in place to take the first steps toward your new goal.

8. In the meantime, tell everyone you know what you are thinking about and ask them for ideas. You never know who may know someone who is doing what you want to do and can help you. Remember that you can take baby steps toward changing your life.

9. Create some affirmations that support you in pursing these goals. Know the universe will always support you when you are clear in your intent. Be aware and thankful of the flow you recognize in your life. The more you flow, the more you allow for flow to take place.

This process can help in gaining clarity on everything in your life. If you want clarity on your relationships, friendships, volunteering, and so on, it is an excellent process to help you get it and be purposeful in your life. It also helps you keep focused on what you love to do. When you are doing things you love, more energy flows to you and from you to the universe.

How Your Energy Works Against You: Energy Blocks

Imagine a fast-running stream, the stream being energy. The stream flows along until it hits a number of boulders. It then has to move around these boulders, thus dispersing its power. The stream's power is compromised because it has to maneuver around the boulders, sending the water in many different directions.

Energy blocks are like huge boulders in your energy fields. These blocks keep you from moving your energy easily and effortlessly toward what you desire. The bigger the blocks are, the less power you will have to create what you desire. These blocks keep you from getting what you want in your life.

Energy blocks exist in the three energetic systems we discussed earlier—the Spiritual, Life Force, and Identity Fields. There are many distinctions within each of these energy fields. As stated earlier, this book will focus only on what you need to know to work with the Success Triad. However, I want to give you a brief overview of our physical energy fields. We can look at the body from the perspective of chi energy, meridian points (which acupuncturists use), or the chakra system. I am trained in the chakra system, and it is the one I most commonly use when working with the physical body.

The Hindu religion has seven major chakras:

First Chakra –   Root; located at the base of the spine; represents physical safety and groundedness

Second Chakra – Sacral; located just above the base of the spine by the belly button and sexual organs; represents our creativity, expression, and sexuality

Third Chakra – Solar plexus; located by the rib cage; represents our power in the world and how we see ourselves

Fourth Chakra – Heart; located in the area of the heart; represents our ability to give and receive love

Fifth Chakra – Throat; located at the base of the neck; represents our connection to spirit and how we express ourselves and speak in the world

Sixth Chakra – Third eye; located in the middle of the forehead; represents our intuitive opening and sight beyond our five senses

Seventh Chakra – Crown; located on the top of the head; represents our connection to the divine

The importance of the chakra system is that understanding it can help you identify issues related to stuck or blocked energy in different parts of your physical body. The chakras give you hints as to what type of issue you are experiencing based on the location of the pain.

What Causes Energy Blocks?

Energy blocks are created in many different ways. They can form in response to a variety of conditions or to a continued cycle of pain in your life. The following are some examples:

- You cannot speak your feelings.
- You hide your emotions.
- You don't feel worthy.
- You are insecure.
- You have suffered a traumatic experience.
- You have been told negative things about yourself, and you believe them.
- You are chained to old energy from a previous lifetime.
- You have felt like an outsider all of your life.
- You hold negative beliefs about yourself.

One of the most common energy blocks is created when you hide your emotions from someone or you don't speak your feelings. When you hide your emotions, the energy behind them has to go somewhere. If, for instance, you stop yourself from crying or expressing sadness, you don't release this negative energy. Therefore, the energy gets stuck, residing in your body.

After a traumatic experience, the brain might shut down, burying the trauma and subsequent emotions somewhere in your body. For instance, have you heard about repressed memories? A repressed memory can be created when a traumatic experience is too overwhelming and the brain decides it cannot and does not want to process it. The brain shuts down and puts the memory in isolation so you don't have to recall the event. However, your body remembers the jolt, fear, and anxiety you may have experienced during the event. When the brain cannot process a trauma, the body stores all the negative energy associated with it.

You carry these blocks in your body and must work harder than usual to move and flow your energy into the universe and to receive energy. Like the stream, your energetic power is dispersed around these energetic blocks, thus weakening your power to create your desired life.

Over years, you may create many small energy blocks in your body or one or two large blocks. When you create energy blocks, the flow of energy through your body may be slow or unfocused. Energy is a form of your power representing who you are in the world and also your expression of what you think and stand for. When you have many energy blocks in your body, you have challenges getting your full self out into the world. You have trouble creating the life you want, the relationships you hope for, and the peace and confidence you may be looking for in life.

The importance of energy-healing work is that it releases these blocks from your body so the energy can flow more easily and consistently throughout your physical body. This will give you even more ability to live the life you want. With your energy flowing unimpeded through your body, you will find it easier to connect to yourself, the universe, and all those around you. This enables you to have greater clarity in your life, which will help you attract what you want to experience.

Think about the last time you had a confrontation with someone. You may have expressed anger, shut down your emotions, or walked out. These tactics all drain your energy. More important, they may create energy blocks in your body that will continue to drain energy for years to come.

Stuck Happens: When Energy Gets Blocked

What does "stuck energy" mean? This is energy that you shove down into your body along with a submerged feeling, belief, or thought. The energy gets stuck because you don't allow yourself to feel, process, or release a past experience. Sometimes, you are conscious of this stuck energy within your body, but most of the time you are not.

Let me share some ways you create your own stuck energy. When I was working in the business world, my specialty was in engineering and customer support services. At the time, this field was mostly male dominated. I was responsible for developing training strategies and programs to support engineers as they learned the latest and greatest technologies. As time went on, I was continuously promoted to higher positions with more responsibilities. At one point, I became a business partner for several business groups simultaneously. This required me to attend weekly, monthly, and quarterly meetings with the vice presidents and management staff of each business unit.

I began to notice heart palpitations when I was sitting in boardrooms or large conference rooms wanting to contribute to the discussion. Sometimes, my palms would get sweaty, or I would begin to hear ringing in my ears. I didn't understand what was happening. I could, at times, move beyond these physical feelings and contribute meaningfully, but other times they were so strong that I couldn't get beyond them. I would sit silently, unable to share my perspective. I could remember a few times in the past when I had felt hesitant to speak up in a group meeting but never to the point of experiencing these sensations.

One day, as I was having heart palpitations and getting sweaty palms, I had a flashback to my younger years. When I was a child, my family used to sit around the dinner table as each of the six children was given five or six minutes to share his or her stories, news, or experiences. My older sisters and brothers always began the process. By the time it was my turn, the fifth in birth order, we were almost through with dinner and everyone was talking over one another, offering information they had forgotten to share when it was their turn or responding to what someone else had to say and preparing to leave the table. I was hardly ever heard. I used to wait patiently for my turn, but most nights it never came. I developed a belief that what I had to say wasn't important. Also, when my parents wanted to do something together as a family, they would almost always defer to the older children's needs or wants, assuming that we younger children would just go along.

As an adult at this large conference room table and being one of the youngest in the room, I was taken back to my childhood dinner table and was immediately experiencing all the stored emotions I had around not being heard. Every time I wanted to speak, I had a physical sensation. My mind kept saying, "Don't bother; no one will listen." This was my mind's way of trying to protect me from reliving those painful experiences at the dinner table.

Until I had this realization, I was unable to identify what was blocking me. I could not release and heal the pain. On an intellectual level, it made no sense that I was having trouble talking to a group; after all, these people were not talking over me or telling me to "shut up." But on an emotional level, the setting—a long table with many people, most of whom were older than me and had more authority than I did—triggered the memories of the long-ago dinner table.

In fact, at that time, if you were to have asked me if, on a conscious level, I had any idea why I experienced anxiety before I spoke, I'm sure I would not have been able to pinpoint it. I may have come up with an explanation of fear that my ideas would not be considered valuable.

This was clearly an unconscious limiting belief (we will talk more about beliefs in the next section) created in childhood, complete with stored energy blocks that caused me to struggle in my adult life. I couldn't stand confidently in my power because it was being dispersed by the energy blocks.

Trying to come up with strategies to move through repressed memories without releasing their negative energy is difficult. So how do you find the stuck energy?

Exercise: Finding and Releasing Stuck Energy in Your Body

Before you start, find a comfortable place to sit or lie down. Light a candle beside you. If you can't (one day I was doing this at the beach, with no candle in sight), imagine placing a lit candle beside you. We will use the candle later in the exercise.

1. Think of a current recurring situation that is unsatisfying or difficult for you. Perhaps it is some pattern that you can't seem to break, such as getting into unsatisfying relationships,

an inability to attract or hold onto a good job, or any other situation in which you are having difficulty getting what you want in your life.

2. Once you have the situation, relive all of the details in your mind. While you are mentally reviewing the situation, see if your body responds with cues of its own. Some typical physical reactions to our thoughts are as follows:

- Tension in different parts of the body
- Discomfort
- Sharp, stabbing pain
- Aches
- Nausea
- Dizziness
- Fuzzy feeling in the brain

3. These are usually symptoms of blocked energy and can tell you where the blocked energy is stored. For instance, when I recalled my childhood dinner table and tried to relive the nightly meals, I quickly started to feel tightness in my throat and a pain in my heart. This makes sense because during the meals my voice was shut down or shut out either by me or by someone else at the table. And I can only imagine the negative stories I made up about why they didn't want to listen to me. These stories probably created some subconscious beliefs that explain the pain I felt in my heart.

4. Cup your hand over the body part that is activated. For instance, I felt all this tightness in my throat when I remembered the dinner table, so I cupped my hand over my throat.

5. Imagine yourself releasing the energy block by pulling the energy out of that spot and placing it into the lit candle. Continue to pull the energy out of the place in the body until you no longer feel any pain, tension, nausea, dizziness, or fuzziness. Energy can be felt in very different ways; sometimes you may feel like you are pulling out a big boulder and other times it will feel soupy or stringy. It doesn't matter what the energy feels like; just imagine pulling it out.

6. When you feel calm in that area of your body, imagine a beautiful white light coming from the universe (or heaven or God), and direct the light into the place in your body from which you pulled out the energy. Once you release energy, there is usually an empty space that should be filled with universal energy, which is supportive energy that makes you feel expansive.

7. As you imagine the white light going into your body, also imagine how you wanted the situation or experience to happen. For example, going back to my dinner table experiences, once I released the energy of the repressed memories, I imagined a dinner table where everyone respected and listened to one another, including me. I also imagined that my ideas and contributions around our dinner table were taken seriously. After releasing the energy I had held in my throat and heart chakras and imagined a different dinner table experience, I totally shifted the way I conducted myself at the boardroom table. I could then engage with the team around the big table without any physical reactions.

When you begin to get insight into how and where you might have stuck energy, follow the exercise above to release it. The most powerful part of the exercise is imagining what you would have wanted to happen instead. This becomes your new, empowering memory and energy in your body.

You may have to repeat step 7 several times because sometimes the pain is very deep or you may have been hurt numerous times. If you have multiple traumas around the same kind of issue, it will take more than one clearing to transform the situation. This was my case with the dinner table. I believe it took a couple of weeks of clearing the energy to notice a shift in the way I responded in the boardroom.

This process is so effective and powerful for releasing stuck energy because energy is stored in our bodies based on our perceptions and beliefs formed from those perceptions. We create our perceptions when something happens to us. We may have perceptions as early as six months old. At that age, we have very little ability to accurately and maturely interpret what occurs in a situation. Many times, we carry around these perceptions of our experiences that hold little to no resemblance to what really occurred. However, if we don't explore these perceptions, we will live in the energy of the hurt, anger, sadness, shutdown, or fear. The energy is stuck in our Energy Systems and physical bodies, and it informs everything we do.

How Do You Know if You Have Stuck Energy?

Energy is a constant, dynamic flow in your body. Your energy is present in every action, reaction, thought, emotion, feeling, and word you express or don't express.

When you are in a positive state, your actions, words, and emotions give you more energy. For example, if you are at a wedding and are dancing, feeling joyous for the couple and interacting with people you know and love, you are very likely to come away from the event feeling energized. Likewise, if you are at work and your manager tells you what a great job you did or acknowledges you for your accomplishments, you are also likely to come away from the experience feeling energized. Positive experiences allow your energy to flow and expand.

Conversely, if you feel that you work tirelessly to get something completed and yet nobody recognizes you for it, you will feel disheartened or upset or even like a failure. These emotions will drain your flow of energy.

You should know that almost every living being has stuck energy. Most people do not go through life without feeling or experiencing some pain or disappointment. Stuck or blocked energy becomes a problem when it affects your ability to live the life you desire. When you feel this happening in your life, it is a great time to work on investigating and releasing stuck energy.

Exercise: Additional Ways to Find Stuck Energy

When you evaluate your Energy System, you must look at all three fields: your Spiritual, Life Force, and Identity Energy Fields. The well-being of all three is vital for you to feel powerful and well balanced in your life.

The questions that follow will enable you to assess the magnitude of your stuck energy. After you ask yourself these questions, you will have more insight into where energy might be stuck (by feeling it in your body) or where you have beliefs that do not support you. After asking yourself the questions below, go back to the energy-releasing exercise on page 38 and apply it.

For *Spiritual Energy,* which is the soul's energy that informs us of the experiences it hopes to have while it is in physical form here on our planet, ask these questions:

- Do I have a sense of a higher purpose for my life?
- Do I have a strong vision of what I desire?
- Am I doing work that fulfills me?
- Do I have relationships that bring joy and fill my heart?
- Do I have a spiritual belief system that sustains me?

For *Life Force Energy,* which is the energy that helps us get out of bed every day and live our lives, follow these steps:

- Imagine that you have a magic wand, and think about what would be your most powerful wish for yourself in the domains of relationships, career, family, money, or whatever life areas are important to you.

- Once you can visualize what you desire most, explore areas in your life where you already have what you want in life.

- Now identify areas of your life where you are not living what you want.

- List the types of thoughts or beliefs you hold that may limit you from realizing your most powerful wish.

For *Identity Energy*, which resides in your physical body and allows access to all your energy, ask these questions:

- Can I feel my energy flowing through my body?
- Are there places in my body where the energy feels stuck?
- Do I feel powerful in my life?
- Do I tend to let life happen to me?
- Do I feel that I deserve what I have in life?
- Do I speak about how I am feeling, or do I stuff down my emotions? (If you stuff your emotions, explore all the ways you do this and why, and determine what beliefs you are holding that don't allow you to speak about your feelings.)
- Do I speak honestly about what is on my mind? (If not, why not? Who do you not speak honestly with?)

Think about how you responded to the above questions, and ask yourself, "Am I creating or do I already have energy blocks in my body around some of my beliefs?" (Hint: Any negative thoughts or beliefs usually have blocked energy associated with them.)

Once you have a list of beliefs or thoughts from the above section, go to the energy-releasing exercise on page 38 and use it to help release these limiting beliefs and thoughts. Remember, the most powerful part of the exercise is imagining what you would have wanted to happen instead. This becomes your new, empowering memory and energy in your body.

How Does Your Energy System Affect Your Moods and Thoughts?

Every single human being has his or her own unique Energy System. Since our energy is made up of our thoughts and actions, it stands to reason that each person's energy will be unique. Our thoughts, beliefs (conscious and unconscious), and actions represent the health of our Energy System. For example, when we meet someone for the first time, we usually quickly judge and assess them. We may do this consciously or unconsciously, but still, we read people and determine who they are based on the energy they put forward.

We usually label people based on our first meetings with them because we read their energy. Following are some labels we use for people:

- High energy
- Low energy
- Pessimistic
- Optimistic
- Negative
- Fun
- Powerful
- Forceful
- Confident
- Engaging
- Standoffish
- Shy
- Bubbly

You could come up with hundreds of labels for people you meet. On what do you base your quick assessment? You may think that it's a logical assessment, but in fact, you are participating in a universal action that for most people remains unconscious.

Your energy extends beyond you in two ways. One is your aura, which is part of your Life Force Energy Field, and the other is your intentional and unintentional thoughts.

Your aura is always out in front of you, anywhere from six inches to two feet. This is where your emotions are stored. If you are a fairly happy, easygoing, and confident individual, your aura holds these qualities. When someone comes up to you and walks into your aura, he or she will feel your energy on an unconscious level and respond to it.

Have you ever had the experience of shaking a person's hand and, in that first greeting, making up your mind about what you think of him or her? You can feel people's energy when you walk into their personal space.

Most people are not conscious of feeling energy; however, they get a good sense of other people immediately upon meeting them. It may manifest as a visceral reaction, a desire to stay connected, or a desire to walk quickly away. You may feel drawn to people because their energy feels good, or you may walk away shortly after meeting them because their energy feels low, negative, or unhealthy.

Thoughts enter your mind almost nonstop throughout the day. Some of your thoughts appear to be random or unintentional, and some are much more intentional. For instance, have you ever thought of a friend or family member you haven't seen in a while, and then the next thing you know, the phone rings and that person is calling you? Our thoughts transmit energy into the universe. If you consciously think about people, you send them energy, and many times they receive it.

You can use your thoughts to make things happen for yourself. I have a client who uses her intentional thoughts about traffic lights to her advantage. Whenever she is in a hurry, she visualizes all of the traffic lights turning green when she arrives at them. Her thoughts go out into the world in an intentional way.

The idea of setting intentions, which we will cover more in the third section of this book about the Manifestation System, is about mastering our thoughts. If we master our thoughts, we create the energy that is most supportive of what we desire.

Your Environment Has Energetic Vibrations

Your Energy System is sensitive and can be affected by things in your physical environment. The Outside Physical System, as I define it, involves places, locations, and objects such as houses, hotels, restaurants, offices, chairs, beds, stones, and other nonliving items.

Have you ever walked into a place and immediately wanted to leave? You may not have known why, but you wanted to turn around and get out of there as quickly as possible. It was probably because you were picking up on some negative energy in the place.

Locations and places hold their own energy and, often, the energy of the people who have passed through them. I recently painted all the rooms in my house in bright, vibrant colors. As a result, I find that I have been neater. It would feel too chaotic for me to live in a space that has the vibrancy of the colors I painted in combination with the energy given off by clutter.

This is an example of color holding a certain energetic vibration. Have you heard about the energetic effects of the color red? It is believed that the color red makes you hungry and also makes you feel like you are in a hurry. Some fast food restaurant chains use red in their packaging, and their dining rooms often have a red decor to promote ordering more food and subliminally encourage customers to leave quickly.

In contrast, have you ever walked into a place and immediately felt at home and had a good feeling? Perhaps it was the way the place was decorated or the objects in the space. When we design our spaces, we attempt to create a certain feeling and usually choose objects and colors to promote that feeling. If we spend time thinking about and engaging in how we set up our personal spaces, we will attract the energy of like-minded people.

Sometimes, when I do intensive energy work with clients, I find I must "smudge" the physical space, which is a way of clearing energy in the room before another person enters. I do this so the energy in my place is neutral; it doesn't hold the energy of the previous person's issues, thoughts, concerns, or energetic releases.

How to Clean a Physical Place

When I first defined *energy* earlier, I said that everything has an energy field. Locations and places, such as houses, hotels, restaurants, and offices, also have energy fields. They hold the energy of the people who are most likely to visit frequently. For instance, if you walk into a fun, high-energy, funky-looking restaurant, most likely the people in the place will reflect this energy through the way they are dressed or act or through their thoughts and beliefs.

Whenever my husband and I go to a restaurant, I know I embarrass him. As the host is seating us, I sometimes know as we are walking to a table that I don't want to sit there; other times, I know as soon as I sit down because I feel uncomfortable and have to move. We ask for a different table three of every five times we go out to dinner. When you work with energy, you become extremely sensitive to the energy in the environment.

Energy in a physical place has a very tangible feeling to it. One of the ways to begin to recognize the energy in a place is to play the Name the Energy game. Wherever you are, take a moment to breathe in the energy of the environment and see if you can name what you are feeling. This will help you to build some distinctions around energy.

Once you have these distinctions, you can become much more adept at recognizing the vibrational energy of a place to determine if it is a good place for you. I recommend that you do this with the energy in your house. If your house or any individual room in it does not reflect how you want it to feel, you may want to examine the thoughts you have in or about your house or the individual rooms. Does the energy of your place reflect your thoughts—positive or negative?

Exercise: Cleaning the Energy of Your Environment

It is possible to clean or cleanse the places we live, work, or visit. There are several ways to clear your environment. I will share with you the two I use most often.

The first is called smudging, and it is done with sage or palo santo (from the Amazon jungle) sticks. I usually smudge my house a few times a year, and I certainly smudge my office daily.

The process of smudging your environment is very simple. You need palo santo sticks or sage smudging bundles. For rooms, follow these steps:

- Begin by lighting your smudge stick and then blow out the fire. You want a smoking smudge stick, not a flaming one. It is the smoke from the smudge stick that clears the energy. (I usually walk around with a candle or lighter because the smudge stick tends to stop smoking.)

- Go to the room you want to smudge and begin in a corner. You can work low to high or high to low. With your intentional thoughts focused on releasing stuck energy, wave your smudge stick in circular motions, imagining the stuck energy releasing. Sometimes you will find yourself lingering in an area of the room with a desire to go over a spot many times. When this happens, it is your intuition calling you to smudge more. Most often it means you have come across stuck energy, and it may take a little bit of time and effort to fully release it.

- Once you have gone around the perimeter of the room, feel free to walk in concentric circles to the middle. When finished, the room may have a slight smell from the sticks or sage bundles, so feel free to open a window. The room should also feel lighter to you.

The second way to clear your environment is to utilize white light and your intentional thoughts.

- Situate yourself in the room you wish to clear. Imagine a big wash of white light coming from universal energy. The white light is pure and has a cleansing ability. Bring in the light with your intentional thoughts, imagining the light washing over the room, cleansing and cleaning any stuck energy.

• The stronger you hold your intentional thoughts about the white light cleaning a room, the stronger and more effective the cleansing energy will become.

I had an experience a few years ago when I went to meet a few former colleagues for lunch. I was talking to one of them at the end of a hallway when, all of the sudden, a door burst open and two people came walking quickly out into the hallway. They were upset with each other ("yelling" under their breath), upset about something that did not go well in their meeting. As they approached me, I started to cough; I continued to cough and cough and couldn't catch my breath. They walked right in front of me and then turned away. I had to run to the ladies room to try to get my breathing under control. I thought I was having an allergic reaction, and I was! I was having a reaction to all the angry energy that had burst out of their meeting room, coming right at me down the hallway. I wasn't prepared for this to happen, and because I am extremely sensitive to energy, I had picked up some of the negative anger energy flow coming from these people. It felt like someone had struck me in the chest with so much force that I couldn't breathe.

Their negative energy had entered my field and consumed all the space around me. I couldn't breathe because I couldn't take in the anger. I canceled my lunch date and headed home. When I could finally breathe again, I calmed myself and realized what had happened.

Now, I am much more careful about being aware of the energy that is around me at all times. I also protect my Energy System and all three energetic fields, which allows me to block unsupportive energy from coming into my fields.

Exercise: Calling the White Light

It's a good practice to protect yourself and your Energy System. There is a lot of energy in our environment, including some that is negative and even harmful. As you start working with energy more and more, it will be important for you to protect yourself from negative Outside Physical System energy attaching to your Energy System. You can do this by using universal light for protection and calling on the energy of the light to place a protective barrier around you and others.

The process I'm going to share with you was taught to me by a shaman years ago. It is a process of calling the white light to me and watching it wrap around me and throughout me to protect me. I visualize this light creating an energetic barrier around me. Once I create this barrier, all negative energy stays on the outside of my Energetic System. This assures me that I will not take in negative energy.

Practice saying the following and imagining the white light flowing through you:

> I am the light.
> The light is within me.
> The light moves throughout me.
> The light surrounds me.
> The light protects me.
> I am the light.

You could instead say a prayer or call in Jesus, Buddha, or another protective spiritual entity. Use something you believe in to surround you and let only good energy flow your way.

I use this to protect myself, my family, and my house, and I always say it when I'm driving. You can flow white protective energy at any time and anywhere you want.

Why Is It Important to Know Your Energy?

Earlier I said that your thoughts and beliefs are tied to your energy. If you become familiar with your energy, you can use it as an indicator of your thoughts and beliefs, particularly unconscious ones. You can examine your thoughts and beliefs to see if they are in alignment based on how your energy manifests.

If you are naturally a high-energy person and you find yourself waking up every day feeling sluggish and with low energy, you can be fairly certain there is something going on. The problem could be happening either consciously or unconsciously. Somewhere within your thoughts and beliefs, something is not aligned with who you are. If you are conscious enough to be able to name which thoughts and beliefs may be getting in your way, you can make decisions on whether you want to hold onto these thoughts and beliefs or are ready to release or shift them.

Your Energy System is complex. I have tried to simplify and focus on the areas of your Energy System that control your reality. Once you become adept at recognizing and shifting your energy to be in support of what you desire in life, you will notice more ease in receiving what you desire. Your energy level or the ability to do things within your day will also increase dramatically. When your energy is aligned and working clearly and cleanly, you will experience more of a sense of peace and well-being. You will begin to see more possibilities and opportunities for yourself because your energy will be clear.

Section 2: Your Belief System

Have you ever heard the saying "you are what you think"? This simple statement holds so much truth. You create your reality by living within your Belief System. This section will answer these questions: What are my beliefs? How can I identify my unconscious beliefs? And, how can I shift them?

The Power of Your Thoughts and Beliefs

What *Are* Beliefs?

Everyone has his or her own Belief System. You created your Belief System based on what you were explicitly told, what you experienced, and what was left unsaid when you were a child. By the age of thirteen, we have about 80 percent of our Belief Systems established. By the time we reach our early twenties, the last 20 percent has become set. Your beliefs dictate the way you live your life. You hold your beliefs as truths, and as long as a belief exists, you will see the world only from that belief. Beliefs can be healthy or unhealthy, serving your life or not.

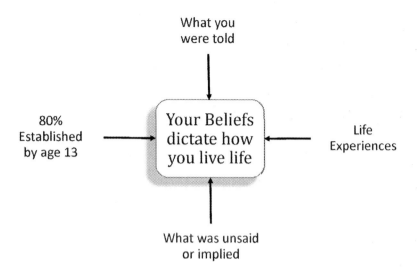

Your beliefs filter what you see and how you experience the world. They shape your life and your ability to respond to what comes into it.

The challenge with Belief Systems is that the majority of the beliefs were developed early in your life and from several different sources. Once beliefs are formed, you rarely go back and examine them to see if they are still the truths from which you consciously want to operate your life. Therefore, much of your Belief System is unconscious. Beliefs were developed so early in your life that you often don't even realize you hold them as beliefs. They feel like "the truth." When we are unconscious of our beliefs, we generally experience things (i.e., situations, people) as good or bad. We make assumptions in life based on our beliefs. We see the world through a certain set of lenses, which either enables us to live the lives we desire or gets in the way.

All of your actions stem from your beliefs. If you developed the majority of your beliefs before you hit your teenage years, your beliefs could easily be the results of skewed, preteen thinking!

For example, I hold the belief that each day has a beginning and an ending. This is my truth because I experience my days this way. The time I see as the beginning changes based on the particular day. For instance, during the workweek, my beginning is at six-thirty in the morning. On weekends, my beginning is at seven-thirty. My belief isn't concerned that the official arrival of a new day occurs at 12:01 a.m. It also doesn't pay attention to the "dawning of the day," which might be at five o'clock. These statements are also the truth, and I know them to be facts. But I know when the day begins *for me*. My belief is what I know to be real. For me, the beginning of a new day is when I wake up.

In this example, you see that beliefs are not about facts. They are what you hold as the truth. Each person's Belief System is unique; there may be some overlaps, but most people's Belief Systems are created from subsets of different sources. You create many different types of beliefs in different ways:

- Cultural beliefs
- Societal beliefs
- Religious beliefs
- Family beliefs
- Gender beliefs

Positive or negative statements that others say to or about you (e.g., parents, teachers, relatives, friends, strangers), your own unspoken beliefs (stories you make up based on what you see, hear, don't see, or don't hear), and your own perceptions of events in your life all combine to form your Belief System.

The following are beliefs many people hold. I point them out because, while they are not scientific fact, many people hold them as if they are:

- "To get ahead, you must work hard."
- "They call it *work* because it's work, not fun."
- "Children today have no respect for their elders."
- "There is never enough time."
- "There is nothing we can do; it has always been like this."

Just suppose for a moment that each of these statements is not a fact but rather a reflection of someone's Belief System. Can you see how changing these beliefs could create a profound shift in one's outlook on life?

Beliefs come in various types, shapes, and outlooks. For one, beliefs can come from your cultural upbringing. If you are American Indian, some of your beliefs will be influenced by your Indian culture. You may practice rituals within your family that were handed down throughout the generations, such as conducting sweat lodge gatherings and honoring Mother Earth.

Beliefs can also come from gender-related messages you received while growing up. Males hold many different beliefs than females. For example, boys are generally taught to compete, while many girls are taught to get along and collaborate. Boys are taught to be aggressive and take charge, but girls receive the message to play nicely and be helpful.

There are family-specific beliefs, religious beliefs, societal beliefs, and political beliefs, to name a few more. When you were growing up, you were influenced by what you were told and what you were taught through many different sources. Some of the sources have a bigger impact on you than others. People's Family Belief Systems are typically the strongest. In this case, you probably either took on the family beliefs as truths or rebelled against them and formed a different set of beliefs as part of your rebellion process.

In both cases, you carried on a lineage of family beliefs from one generation to the next. For example, I asked my friend Dan about his Family Belief System around work. He said he got lots of messages when he was younger about "pushing hard" in life. If something wasn't working, they would just keep pushing harder. There was no belief about examining a situation that is not working and coming up with a new approach. They had to stick to their original plan. Unfortunately, if pushing hard wasn't working, they became stuck because there wasn't an alternative.

This is all too often how it is for most of us. If the belief is working, great; push hard and you get what you want. However, if the belief is not working but you believe it is the truth, it is very hard to shift to a new belief. In Dan's family, there is no room for looking at something in a different way because their old belief is so ingrained. Dan said it wasn't until he realized he had alternative ways to hold beliefs around work that real change began to happen. He explored his Family Belief System and consciously kept the beliefs that helped him in life and worked to release or shift those that hampered him.

Changing family beliefs can be painful, confusing, and often isolating. Discussing or evaluating Belief Systems can be taboo in the family. Everyone in the family operates in a certain way, and no one questions whether this way really serves them. When you begin to shift a family belief, you most likely will be met with resistance from family members who still operate from the ingrained family belief and have issues with your not honoring it.

Client Study

Ann came from a close-knit family that very much supported and loved one another. The family had a strong sense of connection. Everyone got along well, as long as they were operating within the same Belief System. Ann, while working with me, realized that her life was extremely programmed. Her calendar was full months in advance. There was very little room for spontaneity in her life because most of her evenings and weekends were previously scheduled. When she was talking about feeling like she didn't have enough time to do what she loved, I challenged her. How could she have every moment of her life planned and yet be living a life of very little satisfaction?

Ann began to talk about her family culture and how everyone was expected to attend every family event. She was taught to believe that your life was not productive if you were "just sitting around doing nothing." As a result, Ann unconsciously programmed every minute of her life. When we looked at the details of her calendar, we realized that much of what was scheduled were things that felt like obligations or responsibilities, and these were mostly family- or work-related. The family obligations were activities like baby showers, wedding anniversary parties, birthday parties, and so on. The work obligations were various client or employee functions she felt she should attend.

The first job we undertook was identifying and eliminating many of the shoulds in her life. These were areas in which she was doing something because she felt it was the "right thing to do," driven unconsciously from a family belief. One of the biggest beliefs was that if you were invited to an activity or event, you had an obligation to go, or you "should" go. I challenged her to look at her belief and hold it differently. For example, an invitation was just that—an invitation to attend something. It wasn't an order, which was how her family regarded invitations. She decided the old family belief was not serving her and that she wanted to create a new belief. She consciously created a belief that she would attend only events that really interested her. With this new belief in action, she began to give her apologies and drop gifts in the mail instead of attending a baby shower or anniversary party.

What was most interesting for her to notice was that as she started to give her regrets, the people she was giving her regrets to did not seem to mind that she was unable to attend. But her family did mind. They couldn't believe she wasn't going to attend this or that event. One sister angrily called her and told her she was selfish for not going to a baby shower. Ann stuck to her new belief, even in the face of upset and rejection from some family members. She went about scheduling only the things she really wanted to go to or do. As she did this, she became happier and more joyful to be around, and her sisters and brothers began to notice the change. After about six months of living with her new belief, she got a call from the same sister asking if Ann was going to attend a family party that evening. Ann said that she was, and her sister said she wanted to drop off a gift because she had decided she didn't want to go. What a breakthrough!

Ann noticed that her role modeling allowed other members of her family to begin to give up the responsibility or obligations of living their lives by the family "code." Ann not only changed her belief but began to change the Family Belief System. Oftentimes we are so entrenched in our Family Belief Systems that it is hard to see why we can't be happy or have the lives we desire. We must look at our Belief Systems—conscious and unconscious—and keep only the beliefs that support us now and replace those that don't with new beliefs.

A footnote to Ann's family story: Ann's shifting her beliefs, and those of others in the family, away from all the obligations and responsibilities or *should*s created a new sense of freedom and fun within her family. Family members began showing up because they *wanted* to be there rather than felt they had to be there. As a result, the energy of the events tended to be more lively and upbeat.

A Family Belief System is typically the most powerful Belief System. It is developed by watching, listening, and experiencing what goes on around you in your young life. It is rare for parents to sit you down at some point and say "Here is the list of our family's beliefs." Instead, parents demonstrate their beliefs in how they lead their lives. Because of this, family beliefs tend to be unconscious ones.

Client Study

Another example is a client who came to me very perplexed. In every company he joined, he would work hard to get ahead and achieve several promotions, but when it came time to become a senior vice president, he would either leave the company or do something to sabotage his career. Of course, he didn't sabotage himself consciously.

He came to me to find out why he couldn't advance further. He talked to me about how promising his career was at each company and how, after doing well for a while, it would all stop. As he went through his story, I realized that he had a repeating pattern based on an unconscious belief. Consciously, he thought it was about his inability to take on more responsibilities. When I asked him if this explanation really rang true for him, he said no, but he had no other ideas.

I asked more about his history. He talked to me about his early years, growing up with his mother, father, and brother. I asked about his father's success in business. He told me how his dad always says his pride and joy was being able to become a vice president and provide a very comfortable life for the family. This is what defined success for his dad. When I asked him how his dad felt about his (the client's) promotions, he said he was always very proud of him. I asked him how he thought his dad would feel if he succeeded far beyond what his dad was able to do. Without hesitation, he blurted out, "Oh, I couldn't do that. I wouldn't want my dad to think I'm better than him."

In this moment, he got his aha: he was unconsciously holding himself back because he loved his dad and didn't want to hurt him. He had taken on the false or limiting belief that he could achieve only what his dad had achieved to still enjoy his dad's love and support. Later, he had a conversation with his dad about this belief, and his dad told him he was proud of him and loved him no matter what he did in life. He sounded like a great dad; I can see why my client may have developed a belief meant to protect him.

Once my client understood that it was a belief that didn't serve him, we went to work creating new beliefs and visions of how he wanted to be in the future. Within eight months, he became a senior vice president in his company. After a few more years, he left his job and started his own company. I still work with him from time to time, looking at his beliefs and how they may be limiting him as the CEO of his own company.

We will talk more about how to uncover unconscious beliefs later in the chapter.

How Do Your Beliefs Affect Your Day-to-Day Life?

Every day, you face newness. The newness relates to your daily activities, how you choose to show up in the world, and how you interpret what presents itself to you each day.

What are the internal messages you tell yourself as you walk through your day? Do you look at activities, responsibilities, or your daily life as "too much" or "too hard"? Do you look at events as challenges that you are ready and excited to take on? How much energy do you bring into every day? Do you have the belief that you can do anything and therefore know that you will find the energy you need to do what has to be done?

How you answer the above questions really affects how you see your world and what beliefs are operating in your life. Have you ever looked at another person and quickly become tired just thinking about what he or she was accomplishing in life? What are the beliefs that allow one person to take on so much and another person to become overwhelmed by the same amount?

As I told you before, one belief that I had always held as positive was, "I have to work hard to be good at something." My parents instilled a very strong work ethic in each of us, which for me translated into a belief that only if I worked hard could I be successful. I went through life working hard at things. No matter what I undertook, I had to work hard at it. If something came too easily, I didn't trust it to be good.

A couple of years ago, when I was feeling burnt out, a friend asked me, "Why do you work so hard? Why don't you work with ease? Why don't you make everything easy?" This made me ask myself, "Can I meet my goals with ease? Why can't work be about ease?"

This was a new concept. I was almost giddy with the idea of shifting my belief. I realized that I had unconsciously taken on the belief that I had to work hard in order to be good at what I did. But who says this old belief of mine is the truth? That evening, I set out to shift the way I held my beliefs about work having to be hard to validate my worth. I started to affirm for myself the belief that my work was easy.

I suddenly had a huge revelation. I could see how this belief that motivated me to work hard had helped me in the past. It enabled me to focus on my career, to set myself apart from the pack, and to achieve many desired goals in a short number of years. However, it began to hinder me after a while because I had to approach every endeavor from the same "hard" work ethic. This was exhausting. The truth was that *I had outgrown the belief.* I needed a new belief that held a new message that my work would be full of ease and continue successfully with little effort. The old belief, which had once been a friend, had suddenly become a foe. It was no longer helpful unless I wanted to continue being overwhelmed and exhausted.

Exercise: How to Discover and Explore Old Beliefs

1. Think about the various life areas or domains, such as health, money, relationships, career, family, friends, personal development, spiritual development, and so on.

2. List these life areas and rate them on a scale of 1 to 10, where 10 indicates that this life area is very good and feels rewarding and satisfactory. A 10 means you are experiencing exactly what you would like to experience or close to it. A 5 is okay; it means things are going along well—not great, but not bad. And a 1 means that this life area is stalled. You feel dissatisfied, unhappy, or stuck.

3. Select from your list one of the lowest-rated life areas.

4. Ask yourself the following questions:

    - How am I fulfilled by this life area?
    - What about this life area works for me?
    - How am I unfulfilled by this life area?
    - What about this life area isn't working for me?
    - What beliefs am I holding about this life area?
    - Are there any family beliefs around this life area?
    - Are there any cultural beliefs around this life area?

5. Through asking yourself these questions and thinking about the answers, you will probably gain some clarity on beliefs you may be holding that are not allowing you to feel satisfied and fulfilled.

6. Write out these old beliefs in as much detail as possible.

7. Now modify these old beliefs with new beliefs or thought patterns that are supportive of the life you desire. Come up with ways you can think about this area that will give you more energy and open you up to the ability to have what you want. Following are some examples:

    Old belief: I must work hard to get what I want.
    New belief: What I want comes easily and effortlessly to me.

    Old belief: I don't deserve too much happiness. (This is a good one because what is too much?)
    New belief: I deserve exactly what I want in life.

Old belief: If I take too much, there won't be enough to go around.

New belief: The world is full of abundance; the more I take, the more I open up the energy of abundance.

Old belief: I can't change my relationship; it has been this way forever.

New belief: I have the right to have a fulfilling relationship. I can change what I need to make it happen.

Now, using the exercise in the earlier chapter on Finding Stuck Energy, find the stuck energy in your body around the old belief. This is a critical step. In order to embrace a new belief, you want to release the energy of the old belief.

8. Begin to visualize how your new belief shows up in your life. For example, imagine yourself going through your day, thinking your new belief. What will change throughout your day? How will you conduct yourself during the day or during your interactions with others? Imagine showing up in life in this new way. It is like watching a movie: take what you figured out in the above step and see yourself acting, behaving, or receiving your new belief.

9. Finally, create affirmations that will continue to support living in your new beliefs. In the next section, Manifestation Energy, we will talk more about how to define or create affirmations.

Unconscious Beliefs

Early in my career, I bumped into a former colleague whom I hadn't seen in a couple of years. She asked me what I was doing for work. I responded happily, "Would you believe I have this great international job? I get to travel all over the world and work with many cultures!" I said this as if it should be a surprise to her. She responded in a very matter-of-fact way, "Well, you always said you wanted to travel for your work." I walked away feeling a little let down that she didn't seem to appreciate what a big deal this job was for me. Then I realized that because I had told her years ago that this was my intention, it wasn't a big surprise to her. It was just a surprise to me.

I had unconsciously set my intention that the type of work I wanted to do would include traveling. When the job offer came up, I thought it was something totally new and exciting, and I loved the challenges it presented. This scenario of unconsciously setting my intention (and perhaps consciously sharing it lightheartedly with others) has happened over and over again for me. It is a clear example of unconscious beliefs at work. I put my intentions out into the universe, and my unconscious beliefs aligned with the universal energy. Working together, they allowed me to manifest what I wanted in life. This manifestation almost seemed effortless.

With Clarity Comes What You Desire

How are your thoughts affected by your energy and vice versa? Over the years, I started to notice that when I asked my clients what they wanted in life, many of them would respond in detail about what they *didn't* want.

I had a client with whom I worked for several years. When we first started working together, she did exactly that. So I tried to get more specific. For example, I would ask what she wanted in the area of a relationship, and she would say to me, "I know I *don't* want someone who works at different jobs or has children" and so on. I would rephrase the question, and again, she would describe what she didn't want. I proceeded to ask her in every way I could think of what she *wanted,* and after twenty minutes, she finally confessed, with great discomfort, "I guess I don't know what I want." I agreed.

My client had spent all of her energy defining what she didn't want in a relationship. She hadn't focused her thoughts and energy on what she did want.

In energetic terms, if you want to put something out to the universe and you say, "I don't want this, and I don't want that," you will get exactly what you don't want. The universe does not work in the negative, so it will not break down what you don't want. Because all of my client's energy was focused on the negative, the universe assumed that must be what she wanted to experience. The universe best understands *do,* which is a positive.

Whenever you are using universal or divine energy to attract what you want, you must always put your request or intention in terms of what you do want. And be sure to express it as if it is already in your life, as if it has already happened. Why? Because if you ask the universe for something you want, it will respond by helping you experience the situation of wanting, not of having.

Below are some examples of how to improperly and properly affirm what you desire:

Improper: I am tired of not having any money. (The universe will create the experience of you being tired of not having money.)
Proper: I experience abundance in my life, with all the money I need easily flowing to me.

Improper: I want a lover who will both love and respect me for who I am. (The universe will create the experience of you wanting a lover like this.)
Proper: I am in a relationship with a wonderful lover who loves and respects me for who I am.

Improper: I don't want someone who has no time to pay attention to me.
Proper: My relationship is fulfilling, and there is a lot of time and attention for me.

Next, I asked this client, "You are quite clear on who you don't want in your life, so I guess you never get those kinds of people bothering you. Is that correct?" "No!" she yelled with some excitement. "That's *exactly* who shows up!"

When she said this, I knew she had a strong ability to manifest what she wanted, but she was actively sending out a message that was the opposite of what she wanted. We spent the next thirty minutes painstakingly articulating what she wanted in a relationship. After that time, she could clearly say, "I want a relationship based in love that is mutually exclusive, fun," and so on.

Another example involves a friend of mine. We were walking outside, and she was telling me about her husband's job. She said there were three things he never wanted to do in a job, and he focused his job search on never having to do these three things. Well, he was finally hired by a good company and, within months, all three things he had said he didn't want to do suddenly became his responsibilities.

He was so focused in his new job search on what he didn't want that he attracted it right to him. When working with clients who are new to setting their intentions and consciously using their powerful Energy Systems, I give them a simple assignment. I ask them to take a moment when they are driving to a destination that requires parking to ask the universe to provide a great parking space for them when they drive into the parking lot or garage. My clients have never been let down. They will report back to me how they miraculously found amazing parking spots in the optimum locations.

By focusing on what we do want and believing we can have it, we attract it to ourselves. By focusing on what we don't want, we also attract that.

Exercise: Focus on What You Want

Pay attention to what you are focusing on in life. Is it what you *do* want? If so, great; keep focusing on that. Sometimes it takes a while for us to receive what we ask for, so be patient and do not give up hope.

If you are focusing on what you don't want, begin to flip the question around and ask yourself, "What do I want?" Begin to write down the things you want in your life. Say these things to yourself every day. After doing this work, ask yourself, "Do I believe I deserve this?"

Your answer should always be yes. If you find yourself hesitating about what you deserve, ask yourself, "Why shouldn't I have this?"

And then change the question around: "Why should I have this?" You must really believe you deserve. Say to yourself, "Why not me!"

Exercise: Your Purpose Creates Your Goals

1. The first step is to look at all areas of your life and determine what you most want to do, be, or have. For example, if you look at your career, you may say some of the following:

    *   I work part-time.
    *   I make $X per year.
    *   I work in an environment that provides creativity and growth.
    *   I work in an environment where there is consistency.
    *   I travel all over the world.

2. After defining what you want, find a place where you can quiet your mind. Then, enter into a conversation with the universe, telling it exactly what you want. During this step, it is necessary that you express what you want from the belief that you can and will receive it and that you are deserving of it. If you send it out as a joke or with any negative thoughts, words, or energy such as, "I don't want to work in an environment that …," then you will most likely not receive what you want.

3. After you say exactly what you want, take a moment to visualize yourself receiving it. For instance, if you asked to work in a creative environment, visualize what this environment would look like to you, what it would feel like, and how you would behave in it.

4. Let it go. You have now made your intentions known to the universe. Do not stay in a place of desiring or wanting. Move on with your life. Just look for signs that the universe is providing it for you. (And be open to the possibility that they might not be exactly how you thought they would appear.)

What Beliefs Have You Outgrown?

Are you conscious of all the beliefs you hold?

This section is a series of exercises intended to get you to think more consciously about your beliefs. Once you identify them, you'll want to determine which beliefs are friends and which are foes. If they continue to work for you, great; keep them in your life. If they are hindering you, then it is time to show them the door.

Could you identify the top ten beliefs that drive or affect your life the most? I am going to ask you to find them, but please, *do not judge* the beliefs. We are just in the noticing phase. Write down your top ten beliefs.

If identifying your beliefs was challenging, don't worry. By the end of these exercises, you will be clear about which beliefs block you.

Exercise: Getting Rid of Unwanted Beliefs

1. Write down three key phrases that you heard as a child from your parents. For example, I heard the following:

   • Money doesn't grow on trees.

- You have to take care of yourself.
- You can't always get what you want

2. From these phrases, identify the series of beliefs that may have resulted. The ones I wrote down are below, and some of them are still directing my life today. Do these beliefs help me get what I want or support how I want to live my life now?

   - I have to work hard to earn money.
   - Money isn't easy to get.
   - There is a limited amount of money.
   - Don't waste money.
   - I can rely only on myself.
   - I won't let anyone else take care of me.
   - I must always be independent and never let someone else take care of me.
   - I should be happy with what I have.
   - Don't ask for too much.
   - I can't get this, or I can't have that (even before I try).

It is interesting to look at these beliefs. I can see how they have helped me during certain times in my life and how they became hindrances at other times.

Let's examine the beliefs "I can rely only on myself" and "I must always be independent." These worked well for me in my marriage when my husband and I were childless. We both had good careers and financially contributed equally to our home and other things we chose to do. I always felt independent and could decide what I wanted or needed or didn't need but decided to buy anyway.

However, once our triplets were born, I really wanted to stay at home with them for the first few years. This is when my beliefs roared back into my life and became a hindrance. I remember saying to myself, "I can't let Matt become responsible for all of us! I must do my part and earn money. It isn't fair that I am letting someone else take care of me. I am shirking my responsibilities." That's the *short* list of how I was feeling at the time. I was struggling to give myself permission to depend on my husband to take care of us.

I tried to intellectualize my desire to stay home by saying to myself, "I'm doing my part as a stay-at-home mom. I'm taking care of a lot of things for the family." However, at the end of the day, because I wasn't earning a salary, I felt somehow out of sync with how I had always pictured myself. As a result, after about six months of being home with my children, I went back to my high-paying job. I felt better about myself because I was living up to my belief. I was doing my share, and I was independent and could rely on myself again.

After some time of being back at work, I realized that my old beliefs led me to let myself down by not giving me permission to stay at home and enjoy being with my children. This was a time when the strong beliefs I held about myself, which up until that time in my life had really served me, were getting in the way of allowing myself to do what I now most wanted to do. I was doing a disservice by continuing to live in my old beliefs since they didn't allow me to create the life I wanted to live.

Exercise: Top Three Phrases

1. Write down the top three phrases you have heard throughout your life.

2. Once you have the phrases, write down all the beliefs you have created from them.

By now, you should be able to identify more than fifteen beliefs.

Beliefs can be given to you verbally or nonverbally. Have you ever been somewhere with your parents and were just about to do something when you got *the look*? You interpret the look. The look is something that either encourages or discourages you. With the discouraging look, you receive a message to not do something, while the encouraging look conveys that it is okay to do what you want. However, how we translate the energy of the look is left up to us.

We were at a restaurant a few weeks ago with my children. We were waiting to be seated, and one of my daughters reached into the candy bowl to take some candy. She took a rather large handful, and I gave her a look of surprise. She smiled back at me and continued to walk away with the handful. My son, who also had his hand in the bowl, saw my look and dropped all of his extra pieces, walking away with one. The same look was received in two different ways.

This is a good example that demonstrates how we begin early in our lives to interpret the way someone looks at us and the energy those looks hold in our Belief Systems. One child clearly thought it was okay to walk away with a bunch of candy, while the other thought it wasn't. The one who took a handful might already have a belief in place that says, "I can have what I want; it is okay to take what I want." The one who interpreted it as not being okay might hold a belief about "only taking one" as his truth.

Your beliefs are not inherently good or bad. They just exist for you. You can explore your present beliefs as a way of establishing new ones for yourself. This is why it becomes very important to decide which beliefs are beneficial and serve you and your life now and which are old and no longer needed.

Exercise: Releasing Beliefs

There are several ways to change a belief. I provided an exercise earlier in this section that is similar to this one.

Another way to change a belief is by changing the paradigm, or the way in which you look at something. When you do, you can begin to shift longstanding beliefs.

Isolate a belief that you immediately recognize as getting in the way of your doing your work in the world or not helping you the way you think it should. We are going to take this belief through a process so you can notice it, figure out the best thing to do with it mentally, and finally how to *transcend* it, or physically and emotionally move beyond it:

> *Step 1.* Identify one belief you would like to release.
>
> Limiting belief: _____
>
> *Step 2.* Turn the belief around.
>
> Opposite belief: _____

The simplest process is taking what you hold as your belief and looking at its opposite.

Example:

Step 1: Limiting belief: *I need to be independent and rely only on myself.*

Step 2: Opposite belief:

- I can let someone support me.
- I am being supported during this time so I can do a different type of work.
- I make contributions in many different ways.
- I am supported so I can share my unique contributions with my children.

Once I create an exhaustive list, I will go back and look at the beliefs that most serve the life I desire. I will take these beliefs and turn them into a mantra, something I can say to myself over and over that will help support the way I want to be in life.

Following are some examples of mantras I created based on my above new belief:

- I am in gratitude for my husband's desire to support me, and I accept it easily.
- I let the universe and those around me support me so I can live the life I desire.
- I can make requests of others to support me.

Beliefs that encouraged you as a child were typically spoken in the positive:

- You can do anything.
- You can have it all.

- You are going to college.
- You are so smart.
- You are so creative.

The beliefs you hold about yourself now also should be worded in the positive:

- I make up my mind, and I just do it.
- I am always taking action when I need to.

Now look at the limiting belief you wrote in Step 1 above. Ask yourself these questions:

- How is this limiting me or standing in the way of how I want to be in the world?
- What is the opposite of this belief?

Express your new belief in terms that will work for you, that will help you be in the world in the way you want to be.

Now imagine creating a circumstance that is a direct reflection of your living in this new way. Breathe it in. Experience it. Enjoy it. Be clear on what it feels like so you can re-create this feeling in your life. Believe that you truly deserve it and that you can have it.

Now let it go, and let the universe do the work of creating this experience for you. And remember, it might not show up in exactly the way you imagined it. It might come from a person or place you never thought would be your source. If it takes a while to appear, reaffirm to yourself that this is something you truly deserve and remain open and optimistic.

When Beliefs Stand in Your Way

Imagine that you say you want something but that you can't afford it. Then, you get the money to do what you have wanted to do, but you don't do it! That's a moment for you to realize that you may have beliefs standing in your way.

Client Study

A woman I was coaching said, "When I get some money, I will buy a house and have children." Unexpectedly, she got a year's severance package and realized she had the money to buy a house with her husband. However, she couldn't seem to take the necessary steps to do it. He would suggest many different things that they could do with the money, but she never wanted to do any of these things with him. Suddenly, she realized that she had been using the lack of money to keep them in a temporary situation. Their apartment was leased month to month. She saw the pattern of not wanting to make anything permanent with her husband. She and I began to take some action. We began to explore her Belief System around the ideas of permanence, structure, and creating a home.

A lot of her beliefs were unconscious; however, when they began to surface from the work we were doing together, she realized that she was fearful to have a home. In her Belief System, a house was something couples would fight over. She had witnessed an endless array of arguments between her parents over their house. She also realized that a house represented permanence, and permanence was a dirty word to her. Her belief was based on an expression her dad used frequently: "Once you are tied to a house, you can never do anything else, like go away."

This was coming directly from her experiences as a child. These memories shaped her beliefs about what a house represented. She liked the idea of being free, of having a lot of options, and being able to move if she wanted to or change her environment whenever she needed a change.

Once she understood all of her unconscious beliefs, she could begin to change and release them, bringing new, conscious beliefs into her life. For instance, once her husband understood what buying a house represented to her, they stopped fighting over it. This took away her belief that owning a house would always lead to fights. She began to build new beliefs and make healthy associations with owning a house.

But first, she needed to let go of her parents' beliefs and their repeated verbal expressions as being the truth. Second, she had to develop a new truth for herself. She and I began this work by looking at all the possible meanings a house could hold for her. She came up with the following meanings:

- I will be able to use whatever paint I want on the walls in my house.
- I can invest in artwork and not worry about it fitting into the next apartment.
- I can buy furniture to fit the space, not for the convenience of moving it from one temporary apartment to the next.
- I can buy a house that doesn't use up every penny of our income. This would allow us to go on vacations and do things we want to do.

After she and I created these new beliefs, I went into her Energy System and found the energy that was related to the old beliefs. I released this old energy and had her imagine her new beliefs as the new reality for herself.

I am happy to say that they bought a lovely fixer-upper and are having a lot of fun renovating it. Previously, because of her parents' beliefs, she had thought remodeling was a hard and terrible chore. She found out that she not only loves it but actually has a knack for it.

Unconscious Beliefs

The more difficult challenge comes when you are unconscious of your thoughts and beliefs; you just have a feeling via your energy that you are out of sync. I will give you an example.

Recently, I noticed that I was continually correcting and disciplining one of my daughters, which was not part of my normal behavior. I was anxious when we were together. I felt out of sorts and even angry with her. I usually have so much fun with her, but I found myself feeling very heavy and disapproving around her. I would often leave our interactions feeling disappointed in the way I had handled a situation and surprised at my responses.

After sitting with the situation in a very mindful way, what finally became clear to me was that my daughter was demonstrating behaviors I believed to be *wild*. She was, in all her glory, being who she was. She did not care at all what others thought about her taking up too much space in the world or that she had a big personality. She was *so* in the moment of the joy in her experiences. She held a lusciousness about life that allowed her to be present with her feelings and what she wanted to express.

I also discovered my discomfort in her wildness and what I perceived to be the "abandon of her being" in the moment. I began to ask myself, "Why am I so upset by her behavior?" I started examining my own behaviors and realized how much I hold myself back, not letting myself live and express fully every day. I uncovered a set of beliefs from which I was operating that controlled how I managed myself in the world:

- What others think is more important than how I feel.
- I shouldn't bring too much attention to myself.
- It isn't safe or right to be so wild with my emotions and my personality.

Since I uncovered these unconscious beliefs, I no longer want to live within their constrictions. They were clearly passed down to me to control my behavior as a child. I began to more consciously think about what was acceptable for me and how I wanted to interact and be in the world. I used my daughter as a model for myself to be fully engaged in the moment and let myself fully shine.

Exercise: Uncovering Unconscious Beliefs

There are several ways of finding unconscious beliefs. Unconscious beliefs are usually behind these situations:

- You feel stuck.
- Someone's behavior is really bothering you.
- You have a desire to be one way in the world and yet you can't live from that place.
- You have a lot of negative self-talk or censorship around your own actions. (Usually you are measuring yourself against someone else's standards and taking them on as your own or you are controlling how you appear based on someone else's beliefs.)

Once you uncover your unconscious beliefs, you can do the following:

- Release the energy of the belief (see previous exercises).
- Think about how you want to be in the world.
- Create new beliefs that support the way you want to be.

Summary

In this section, we have examined how conscious and unconscious beliefs can get in your way and how to change your beliefs to better create the life you want to live.

The most difficult lesson regarding Belief Systems is that you take your beliefs for granted and sometimes can't even see them as beliefs. The strongest ones are usually the most invisible. You hold them as self-evident truths.

The best way to correct this is to start recognizing the aspects of your life that are not working the way you want them to. The next step is to see if there are any hidden beliefs that may be enabling this situation.

Next, imagine changing those beliefs into something you can truly believe and that will also realistically work for you. Set your sights high! You were not meant to live a mediocre, vaguely unhappy life. The final step is to own your new beliefs and use daily affirmations to firmly replace the old beliefs with the new ones.

Section 3: Your Manifestation System

Manifestation Energy is the ability of an individual to co-create with the universe exactly the life he or she desires. The more powerful people are in co-creation, the more evident it becomes in their lives. Manifestation Energy is affected by your Energy and Belief Systems and also by your readiness to receive. In order to create a strong Manifestation Energy, you need to focus on several factors in your life:

- Intentions – the level of clarity and passion you hold about your desires
- Receiving – the ability to accept what you are asking for
- Belief – the ability to genuinely believe you can have what you want
- Energy and focus – continuing to make the request, sending positive energy to the universe, and being open to what shows up

Intentions

In the late eighties, I was working with my spiritual mentor when he mentioned the use of intentions and how our intentions transform into energy matter. Energy matter is what is created when our thoughts turn into energy. This energy matter travels in universal light, informing the universe of what we desire. The universal light helps us to manifest whatever we desire. The more focused and positive our energy matter is, the easier it is for the universe to provide it to us.

When you set your intentions, it is like writing a letter to the universe, stamping it, and sending it through universal light. The universe answers all letters. The answers typically show up in opportunities and possibilities for you to step into the intentions you requested.

In over twenty years of coaching others, I have taught many clients how to set their intentions as a primary way to dramatically shift and change their lives. My clients and I have seen remarkable results. Now, I would like to share this technique with you.

My intention in writing this book is to empower you with the full use of your intentions. It's important for you to know how, where, and when to use intentions. I use them in several different ways in my life. Just like when I make plans for my business and need to consider long- and short-term goals, I can plan my life using my intentions, considering long- and short-term desires.

What Are Intentions?

Intentions are the statements in which you declare what you want in your life. Intentions state what you want to experience and how you want to bring forth those experiences. Intentions are successful when you are clear on what you want and how you want to be in life. The clearer you are, the easier it is for you to have success with your intentions. You will learn more about clarity later in the section.

Intentions must be put out into the universe with the following beliefs:

- You can have what you want.
- You are worthy of what you are asking for.
- You absolutely feel this intention is real.
- You are ready to receive it.

This is why we worked on beliefs in a previous section of this book. Your beliefs need to be aligned with your intentions, or you will end up sabotaging yourself.

Finally, you must feel the energy of your intentions and send it out to the universe. It is not enough to say you want something. You must really become clear on what you want and ask the universe, almost with a forcefulness, to send it to you. The more passion, desire, and excitement you have about your intention, the more energy you hold around the intention and the faster it will come to you.

Intentions can be sent out for almost anything. For instance, one client had to give a big presentation. I told her to send into the universe exactly what she wanted to experience in the presentation and to visualize the response of the attendees. She asked the universe for help in delivering a funny, insightful, and intelligent presentation that raised people's awareness and interest enough that they would all want to commit to supporting her project. When she finished her presentation, she had achieved exactly the outcome she was looking for both in terms of how she presented and how the attendees responded.

Client Study

I had a client who created intentions to move from a European country back to the United States. He had several different fears of moving back, such as not being able to find the right place to live, not finding the right job, and having to deal with all his family's unfinished business. A simple move can overwhelm anyone, but he had additional concerns about finding a new job in the States after being out of the country for most of his adult life and facing all the complicated family issues. He became paralyzed with fear.

We worked on taking one step at a time. The first step was helping him become very clear about why he was moving back. He listed all of the positive reasons for the move. Once he could clearly see that his positive reasons outweighed his fears, it freed him up and also provided another very important element. He was then able to be clear about setting his intentions and asking the universe to support him.

The next step was tackling his fear around finding a job in the United States. His biggest issue was his belief that he didn't know anyone who could help him find one. Networking held a strong negative energy for him. He felt that he had been out of the country so long that he no longer had contacts in his industry. We went to work on getting clear about the type of work he wanted to do. He also had a concern about work-life balance since companies in Europe had a stronger commitment to this than those in the United States and provided many more family benefits.

I had him make a list of the companies in his industry that were known for good work-life balance. He began to survey his current coworkers and colleagues to see if they had connections in any of these companies. After reaching out to many people and also waking up every day with a set of clear intentions, he landed a key contact that helped him get an exciting job in a company that met his needs around work-life balance.

The principle of setting your intention is first and foremost about clarity. If you become clear on your intention and stay focused on inviting it in, you are halfway to success. The other two principles are asking the universe to aid you in receiving your desires and then moving into action to support your desires.

How Do You Ask the Universe?

There are many different ways to request that your intentions be supported and fulfilled by the universe. However, I have found that the most successful way to send out your intention is to really feel it, tell the universe with conviction that you want it, and ensure that your Belief System is aligned and ready to receive.

Exercise: Creating Intentions to Manifest What You Desire

Creating your intentions can be done in three easy steps:

1. Visualize – Dream it, feel it as real now; create the seed

2. Hold your intentions – Create your hope statement; desire lives here

3. Affirmations – Make verbal statements that create a bridge from within you to the outside physical world; beliefs live here and can be changed here

Step 1: Visualization

Visualization is a critically important step. If you can't imagine something, you can't allow it in. You can say you have a desire to have certain things in your life or that you want things to be a particular way, but if you can't see it, feel it, and hold it as true for you, it becomes very difficult to achieve.

After you are clear on what you want to be, do, or have in life, begin to imagine your life as if you have it now. If you had what you desired *right now*, what thoughts would you have, how you would feel, and what might you be doing?

The more you visualize yourself in the state of having what you are requesting, the easier it is to bring it to you. Do this step in the exercise every day. For example, when I need to move to a new office, I begin to visualize months in advance the type of new space I desire. I do this by imagining myself walking into the new space to go to work. I imagine myself holding workshops and seminars in my new space. I see myself printing up new business cards and stationery to reflect my new address. The more I visualize, the clearer and more consistent I become around my request to the universe to provide me with the exact office space I desire. When I eventually start the search for a new office space, which can be months later, I never have trouble finding one that meets my needs.

Step 2: Holding your intentions

When you have a visual associated with your intention and a solid and strong feeling for what you desire, create a clear, succinct statement about what you desire. This may be a broad, overarching statement, but when you visualize it, you will want to add as much detail as possible.

One intention statement I created for my new office space was, "To have a large, light-filled space where my clients feel good and comfortable." When I visualize this intention, I may imagine more details such as the type of windows, the colors on the wall, the number of rooms, the thickness of the rugs, and the storage space in the new office.

Step 3: Affirmations

This step involves creating powerful affirmations to help you overcome beliefs you may have that are blocking the intention. With my new office space, I had a limiting belief about finding the space in a location that was affordable and close to my home and my clients. I found a location that was perfect for me and my clients but was generally considered more expensive. I started to believe that I could not find an office space in this town because it would be out of my budget. So, I wrote an affirmation to help counter this limiting belief: "I easily find the perfect space in the town I want that is affordable and in a location central to my home and clients."

Affirmations are used to help you shift your beliefs. If you say the affirmations enough with genuine feeling, it is possible to shift your thoughts, which can shift your beliefs. Also, by saying affirmations regularly, you remind the universe of what you desire.

When working with affirmations, you must be very conscious of your beliefs. If you use affirmations to help change a belief and you find yourself shifting the way you think about it, you know the affirmation is working. However, if the belief is deeply rooted in your values, you may need to do some of the shifting belief exercises described in Section 2.

Client Study

I worked with a client who wanted to attract a husband. She had been dating for years with no success. We worked together on clarity first—what she wanted in a man.

She began to visualize the man, created a clear intention, and finally wrote some affirmations to support her in believing she deserved this man in her life. Several men showed up on her radar screen right away. But before she had the opportunity to go out with them, she would immediately focus on why things wouldn't work out with each man. She would not even pursue these possible relationships.

After I had witnessed her exhibiting this behavior twice, I started to question her about her beliefs about herself. Did she feel she was worthy to have a great relationship with a man in her life? Did she really want what she said she wanted, or did she want some other type of man? Interestingly, she confessed that she actually had already experienced long-term relationships with two men who fit the profile for the type of man she wanted, but neither of the relationships had worked. After much questioning, we discovered that she felt she could attract the type of man she wanted but that she had some beliefs that it would never work out. She had a set of very strong unconscious beliefs about not being good enough for this type of man; she thought, "He will leave me once he gets to know me."

Once we uncovered her unconscious beliefs, we could do something about them. We worked with her unconscious fears that were blocking her desires.

Return with me for a moment to the Belief System section. Remember that when you begin the belief work, you have to search for the unconscious beliefs that are blocking you from getting what you say you want. Clearly, this client had a few. We identified them, found the energy in her body, and released it. In her case, the energy centered on these two past unsuccessful relationships that left her feeling like a failure. She also had energy stored in her body that held the belief that she was unlovable.

Once this client and I mined the unconscious beliefs and made them conscious, we cleared them from both the Energy and the Belief Systems and used the Manifestation System to send a clear and clean message to the universe. She was able to create new beliefs, bringing fresh energy and new affirmations that reflected the truth, affirming that she was absolutely lovable and deserving of this type of man. Within three months, she met someone whom she later married.

No matter what you do on the conscious level, if you have unconscious beliefs and have energy tied to them, they will affect your ability to step into your intention and to get what you desire. If you begin to notice that you are not getting what you desire, you probably have some unconscious beliefs firmly planted in your energy and transmitting a conflicting message to the universe. The clarity that is so important to have when sending intentions into the universe becomes muddled. You must use the exercises in Sections 1 and 2 to clear unconscious beliefs and energy from your systems.

When You Think You Aren't Getting What You've Asked For

By setting intentions, you allow the universe to partner with you and help you achieve what you want. You might say to me, "Well, I put my intention out to the universe, but I didn't receive what I asked for." Several things may be going on.

You actually may have received your request; however, it may not have shown up the way you expected it to. Or you may not have been ready to receive what you requested for reasons that are not available to you right now. It's also possible that you were holding a stronger limiting belief that was conflicting with the intention and that didn't allow you to be fully open to seeing or receiving it.

I have talked about how limiting beliefs can get in your way. Now, let's talk how intentions are sometimes responded to and answered but not in the exact packages we requested.

You can ask all day long for an intention to be answered; however, if you don't believe in it or can't receive it, you will not see it when it shows up. Because of your powerful Belief System, you must try to be as aware as possible about how you really feel about your intention or request. You should spend time exploring the possibility of having conscious or unconscious limiting beliefs that may prevent you from receiving what you desire.

Client Study

I worked with a client who went through a difficult divorce. A couple of years afterward, she told me she was ready to meet the man of her dreams, and I asked her to describe who she wanted. She came back to me with a checklist. At the top were general characteristics: kind, considerate, funny, loving, committed, and so on. The next part of the checklist was a very detailed description of how the partner she was trying to attract must look and act, the worldly possessions she expected he would have, as well as the things she did not want him to have. For instance, she was looking for someone who was unmarried; if there were children, they needed to be old enough to be living outside of the house. There could be no fiscal obligations to anyone else ... and the list went on.

I didn't think that this client was ready to meet a man. In her list, she went beyond the essence of what she wanted in a man and a relationship. She even weighted and scored each checklist item to indicate which "qualifications" were most important.

One year later, she met a man. It wasn't that it took her a year to find someone to meet her criteria; it took her a year to understand the reason she had so many rigid ideas about her dream man. She held a belief that she wouldn't be hurt by a man who could meet all her expectations. Once she grasped the idea that even if a man met every criterion on her checklist, she might still get hurt, she began to let go of all of her "requirements."

Another belief we uncovered was that she didn't trust her judgment in knowing if someone was good for her. As we explored what she needed and wanted and she gained confidence about the person she was, she realized that she could trust herself to recognize what was good for her. Her checklist went from 150 items to the 10 most important qualities she hoped her future mate would possess.

Within just weeks, a man showed up. This man would never have met even the first few requirements of her old list. He was in the process of getting divorced, still officially married, and had children aged two and four. He was debt-tied to his ex-wife: they shared a business together. All of these things would have eliminated him earlier. However, this man did fit her new, clarified Top Ten list. I am happy to say that three years later, they are married with a child on the way.

Remember, when sending out your intentions, *be clear and send out the spirit of the intention.* For example, you could say, "Universe, please send me a man with whom I can be intimate, a man who is trusting, fun, loving, able to share and communicate, and to whom I am attracted."

On rare occasions, we ask for personal things that we believe will bring us happiness, joy, or fulfillment. The universe, however, has a broader perspective than we do and may know that some aspect of what we seek is not in our best interest at a particular time in the way we seek it.

Client Study

One winter, we became co-owners of a mountainside condo with another family. It was clear to us that the condo was adequate for the moment, but as our children grew, the bedroom situation would no longer work. After owning it for only one season and anticipating the future problems, we decided to sell it to buy a bigger place. The prices for larger condos had dropped, making them easier to afford. We all set our intention and waited to see what happened.

While our place was on the market, our ambivalence became clear: although we would need a larger place when our children got older, did we really need to move right then? We were vacillating on the difference in cost. Not only would the new condo we were considering cost almost

25 percent more than the one we were in, but it also needed about thirty to forty thousand dollars in renovations. Considering our uncertainty and not getting the price we wanted for our current condo, we decided to wait.

Four months later, I was sitting at the beach when I got a call from a realtor in Maine. She said she had a buyer for our current condo. I told her it wasn't on the market, and she said she had the perfect, larger condo that did not require much work with motivated sellers ready to make a deal. We gave her the go-ahead to show our place. We immediately received a very good offer, prompting us to look at the larger condo she had suggested. It was perfect for us in all ways but price. After some discussion, the realtor decided not to take her commission on the sale of our current condo to allow the people who had made the offer to afford it and also save us money that we could then apply to the offer on the larger condo, which was accepted by the owners.

Interestingly, everyone benefitted: the buyers of our condo got an amazing unit at a price far below market value due to the realtor's forfeiting her commission; we got a bigger, better unit with affordable finances; and the owners of our new unit were eager and able to move on. We had found our bigger place for less money than we ever imagined.

When we had first taken our condo off the market in the spring, we had all felt a little deflated. We thought our intentions to buy a bigger place hadn't manifested. My friend asked me at the time why I thought things hadn't worked out, and I told her that I thought it was connected to our ambivalence about needing a new place right away. In this example, energetically speaking, we had done all the things we needed to do to make something happen, but it was not the right thing for us. The universe needed more time to deliver to us a more harmonious situation.

Long-Term and Short-Term Intentions

Long-term intentions reflect the "big picture" of what you desire for your life. For example, one of my long-term intentions is that I am able to continue on my healing path, learning and sharing what I discover with others. This intention manifests in my life in several ways. I work with clients one-on-one to help heal them. I lead workshops to help people live *into* their full potential. I'm the director of an energy-healing school that helps others learn the techniques and processes I use to shift energy and heal. Long-term intentions are broad, and within them you can take multiple actions to support your desire.

Your short-term intentions are concerned with choices for today, like an upcoming meeting or interaction. For example, when I get my children off the school bus, my intention is to have meaningful interactions with them. I want to be present to their needs and desires. Because this is my intention, when they get off the bus and want to do things that weren't planned, it doesn't upset me. I remain in the energy of staying present to what they need. Our afternoons go by with very little stress because I am not trying to make the "right" things happen. I am in alignment with my children's energy and desires.

Reaching Your Goals

I once saw an interview with Jim Carrey, the comedic actor, and he told the interviewer that he had always known he was going to be famous. He had held the vision of himself becoming a well-known actor from the time he was very little. He used to walk around with a hundred dollar bill in his wallet so that even when he couldn't afford his rent, he could always feel that he was in abundance. He held a very strong and clear intention about his life and career, and it came to fruition. Unlike us, Jim didn't have to pick out the wrong condo and think it was the one for him. He knew he had only to wait and his desire would manifest.

Summary

Setting your intention is a powerful way to directly establish your communication and relationship with the universe. When you practice being clear and succinct in sending your requests out to the universe, pay attention. Typically your requests will be handled quickly! Also, the more frequently you make requests of the universe, the stronger your relationship with it will become. The universe will grow more familiar with you and you with it.

When you drive to a favorite store or visit a family member, you are familiar with the route. You get into your car, and it is easy to get there smoothly and quickly. You don't need maps to find your way. It is the same when working with universal energy; the more you are in relationship with the energy, the more it can flow directly into you.